ACKNOWLEDGMENTS

This book is dedicated to the memory of my late wife, Mary, a woman who loved me and who was my best friend for nearly 40 years.

I wish to acknowledge those who helped me bring this book to you. Thanks to my brother, Edward Girard, for his encouragement. All my adult children, my grandchildren, and my great-grandchildren for their love and support. To the Mayor of Thornton, IL, and all those who work at the village hall. Thanks to all the staff and officers of the Thornton Police Department. To the officers of the Homewood, IL, Police Department, who showed their support. And thanks to the members of the Lake County Indiana Sheriff's Pipe and Drum Band, who supported me.

I also wish to thank Pastor Michael Hoggard of Bethel Church for his contribution and his teachings that opened my eyes, enabling me to discover that which I share with you in this book. And finally, a very special thanks to a very special person, my good friend Darllynne Michael, who spent the time in editing and insights she contributed.

May God bless each and every one for their contribution.

TIMES UP!

TIMES UP!

World Ahead Press is a division of WND Books. The views and opinions expressed in this book are those of the author and do not necessarily reflect the official policy or position or WND Books.

Paperback ISBN: 978-1-944212-02-5
eBook ISBN: 978-1-944212-03-2

Printed in the United States of America
16 17 18 19 20 21 XXX 9 8 7 6 5 4 3 2 1

FOREWORD

The writing of a book like this one requires more basic research than I believe is possible for any one mortal human being. While there is a considerable amount of original material in this book, much of the research has been done by others. I have drawn upon the efforts of many authors who have written books on different aspects of the conspiracy.

This conspiracy can be compared to a jigsaw puzzle. When you open the puzzle box and dump out its contents on the table, all you see is a lot of little pieces, but when you finally put all the pieces together you usually have a beautiful picture. I have tried to put all the pieces together. To my knowledge, there is no other book until now that does that. I want to warn you, though, when we get done we will not have a beautiful picture.

I owe a deep debt of gratitude to each of these authors who put hundreds of hours of research into each piece of the puzzle about which they wrote. I could not have written this book without them.

I also want to acknowledge my own inadequacy. I look to God for His wisdom, understanding, and guidance.

> "And he said unto me, My grace is sufficient for thee: for my strength is made perfect in weakness. Most gladly therefore will I rather glory in my infirmities, that the power of Christ may rest upon me" (2 Cor. 12:9).

> "I can do all things through Christ who strengthens me" (Phil. 4:13).

CONTENTS

CHAPTER ONE

OUR DAYS ARE NUMBERED

Jesus is coming tomorrow. Wow, that's a profound statement. You're probably thinking, are you a date-setter? I was told of a person who had an old barn, which he converted into a tavern. After a week or two, he became very concerned because he was only drawing in two or three people a day. Then he came up with an idea that he believed would draw a large crowd. He took out a bucket of paint and painted in bold, large letters, FREE BEER TOMORROW, it worked. The next day he couldn't handle the crowd by himself and immediately hired three people on the spot to help with the crowd. When anyone would ask about the free beer, he would tell them to read the sign outside.

Just as in my opening paragraph, one day that statement about Jesus will be right. This writing is generated by that thought. There are many who are seeing the things that are happening in our world, and don't understand what's going on. Perhaps they have an unopened book in their homes that address those very issues. The book, of course, is the Bible. We Christians, when seeing these things, shake our heads and think, *I thought Jesus would be back before that happened* as we watch Scriptures unfolding before our eyes. On the other hand, like so many other authors, we are happy that we have the opportunity to warn others, reaching out to them with the Gospel of Jesus Christ. People need their eyes opened to just what's going on.

What if I told you such things as the makeup of man and the description of the church are alike? How about if I told you that there is a picture of 9/11 in the Bible which actually seems to point to that date? We will be looking at those things and much more, which I think will astonish you. In the Bible there are approximately five thousand times that make mention to a certain period of time. All forms of the word *number* are found over three hundred times. This does not include the actual mention of numbers used, such as, "3 days" or "40 days" or mentioning the size of the ark or the size of an army and so forth; in other words, the mathematics of various things. This would add thousands of times numbers are used. God even knows the numbers of hairs on your head. I had to address those things as they are important to know as we proceed.

God wants us to know and be ready for Him when He returns, which is the reason for this book, and so many more that seem to point to His soon return. I found some things that are happening in the here and now that parallel with Scriptures that should make us realize where we are concerning to what is happening. The gospels, such as in Matthew chapters 24 and 25, Mark chapter 13, and in Luke's Gospel, chapters 17 and 21 give us warnings from Jesus that tell us of things that will happen just prior to His return. There are thousands of verses throughout the Bible that give us a clear warning. In the following chapters of this book, I will show you our recent history, and the Scriptures which tell us that we should learn from and show us where we are in the prophetic time clock. I will also show you when that clock started ticking.

I think I may have taken some liberties insofar as showing some of the dates I found, but on the other hand, I believe I was spot on. What we will be looking at doesn't change the exciting prophecies that are recorded throughout Scriptures. What I think I found shows us just how awesome our God is. I don't believe there has been another author who has come up with these concepts. It is not my intention to add anything to the Scriptures or take anything away. I did find this study interesting and somewhat of an eye-opener.

I was a police officer for over thirty-five years before I finally retired, so I approached this study as "looking for clues" in the Bible. Now I serve as chaplain for the Homewood police, and the Thornton police and fire departments in Illinois, and also for the Lake County Indiana Sheriffs Pipe and Drum band, and I hope I can encourage my fellow officers and firefighters who put their lives on the line every day to find the same Jesus, the Lord and Savior of our lives. Not just a thought of the Jesus who was, but of the Jesus who is alive and doing things. I'm talking about a real relationship. After all, He put his life on the line for all of us.

Again, going back to the main topic of time and numbers, what I found to be so interesting was the use of numbers tied so closely to our lives, in most everything we do. How far off could that dreaded number 666 be? I can barely recognize the United States of my childhood as so much has changed. Again, numbers and time have much to do with everything.

I found that numbers are practiced in numerology and astrology dating back to the seventh century, when the Arabs conquered the northwest Indian subcontinent, where they learned of Indian mathematics and astronomy. They also learned of other combinatorial mathematics, such as the magic square.

The above picture, an iron plate, is an order six magic square in Arabic numbers from China dating back to the Yuan Dynasty. Pictured below is an example of what is considered a magic square that you may recognize.

2	7	6	→15
9	5	1	→15
4	3	8	→15

15   15   15   15   15

An order six magic square derives from a mathematical equation. (See Wikipedia for more information.) These types of boxes with numbers were used in astrology, fortune telling, and other types of worship. There are many types of these numerical boxed mathematics that have to do with months of the year and so on.

In fact, this magic square used in the Yuan Dynasty is being used worldwide on the internet and in puzzle game books under the guise of a brain-game called *Sudoku*. You will find nine numbered cubes in a 9 x 9 number cube configuration in varying degrees of difficulty. Much time can be lost, as a person may not end their quest to solve the puzzle for hours or even days and weeks. You will also find later in this book the significance of the number 9.

As it turns out, Benjamin Franklin was deeply involved in this practice and also had great skill in the construction of magic squares, as he was deeply involved in astrology. It's believed that Thomas Jefferson also had the same thoughts on this subject.

As Thomas Jefferson said in his inaugural address, they were "enlightened by a benign religion, professed indeed and practiced in various forms, yet all of them inculcating honesty, truth, temperance, gratitude, and the love of man, acknowledging and adoring an overruling, and Providence, which, all its dispensations, proves that it delights in the happiness of man here, and his greater happiness hereafter."

What lead me to these historical figures was my search of numbers and the many ways they're used in everyday life, such as on our currency. I'm not talking of the number relating to the size, or the dollar amount. I'm talking of the hidden numbers and also the hidden messages on the dollar, such as words and symbols, et cetera.

I found in my personal library a book that I had and almost forgotten entitled, *The Great Seal of the United States* by Paul Foster Case (copyright 1935). He lived from October 3, 1884 to March 2, 1954. Mr. Case was heavily involved in the occult before and after he became a mason. He wrote a number of books on the occult practices that were published, one of which was *The Great Seal*. In this book it says, "***This nation* [our United States] *was inspired from the Hebrew and Christian Scripture, and from the doctrines of* Pythagoras, Plato, the Alexandrian School, the Kabbalists and the Rosicrucians."** (emphasis mine)

The book continues, "*The Holy Bible rests open on the altar of every American lodge. It is the* Great Light *which rules and guides the Craft in faith and practice. In its pages are found those conceptions of God, Man and the Universe which were briefly proclaimed in the Declaration of Independence, more explicitly worked out in the Constitution, and most admirably symbolized by the seal of the United States.*" In that portion above that I have emphasized with italics, who is the Great Light he is referring to in his mind? There is only **one true light**, and that is **Jesus**, who is the **light of the world**. (John 8:12) What does that Craft, with a capital *C*, stand for? It doesn't stand for Christianity, which also has a capital *C*; otherwise, it would have been mentioned.

Now I would like to discuss some numbers, and one number in particular which is repeated on the dollar bill. That number is 13 which is all over our one-dollar bill. This number is associated with evil. Nimrod, mentioned in the Bible, was an evil man. He was the thirteenth descendant from Adam. The dragon, describing the devil, is found 13 times in the Book of Revelation. In the 13th chapter of Genesis we find the first mention of Sodom.

Looking at the above, let's first look at the back side of the dollar, where we find 13 arrows in one of the talons of the eagle. In the opposite talon we see a branch with 13 leaves, which is supposed to represent an olive branch. In this same branch you will also find 13 olive berries. In the shield over the breast of the eagle are 13 stripes. Over the eagle's head are 13 stars. The right wing of the eagle has 32 feathers, the left wing 33. That's 5 x 13 = 65. In the beak of the eagle is a banner which reads, *E PLURIBUS UNUM*, which translated says "out of many one." In this Latin phrase are 13 letters. Around the stars above the head of the eagle are a circle of 19 clouds. Inside those clouds and just outside the stars are found what is supposed to represent glory, or 24 divisions of glory. Adding the 9 tail feathers to the 19 and the 24 comes to 52, or 4 times 13. If you're still with me, altogether we have 15 times accounted for where the number 13 is found. That is found in just one of the two seals.

Do we dare look at the other seal? Looking above the pyramid, we find *ANNULT COEPTIS*, which contains 13 letters. The words mean "He has prospered our undertaking." If you read the last three words of this paragraph, you'll see just what that undertaking is. The date on the base is written in Roman numerals, (for a reason). The reason is they add up to 9 letters. These numbers are pretty much where the 9 tail feathers of the eagle are found. Under the Roman numerals is found the phrase *NOVUS ORDO SECLORUM*, a phrase of 17 letters. Adding the 9 letters (Roman numerals) under the pyramid and the 17 and the top 13 comes to 39 letters. That is 13 times 3. The words below, giving one word at a time, *NOVUS*, is the word for **new**, *ORDO*, is the word for **order** and *SECLORUM* is the word from which we get **secular** or **worldly** or **world**. In essence, the phrase is saying or meaning a *NEW WORLD ORDER*.

If you count the rows on the pyramid, you will find, of course, 13. No surprise there. Above the pyramid, what they call the Eye of Providence is the Egyptian eye of Horus. What else would be above an Egyptian pyramid? If you look closely at the eye, it appears to be a reptilian eye. Wasn't it the serpent that tempted Eve in the garden? Satan is always opposite of God maybe that's why He is the capstone. Ephesians 2:20 and 1 Peter 2:6 both refer to Jesus Christ as the chief cornerstone, the foundation. This capstone tries to exalt Satan over all, and this has nothing to do with the God of our Bible. I came up with 19 times that we find this satanic number 13 showing up, which I found to be interesting, as that's how many satanic terrorists were on those four high- jacked planes on 9/11. I will show you more on the 9/11 attack later, where you will see how the number is used, for instance the phrase *New York City* has 11 letters. New York was the eleventh state to join the union. The name *George W. B*ush as 11 letters. The word *Afghanistan* has 11 letters. Flight 77 struck the Pentagon; that has 11 letters. On **9/11**, 1941, there was a ceremony at which the cornerstone for the Pentagon was laid. We will look at this more closely a bit later.

For now, we"re looking at the dollar and the number 13. The phrase "Don't tread on me" has 13 letters. "The Spirit of 76," once again 13 is found. The numbers 7 and 6 added together total 13. July the Fourth has 13 letters. These things just don't happen. They are well thought out, like the magic squares. Much of what I'm discussing of these symbols, numbers, and words on our currency have been mentioned in other writings, documentaries, perhaps even on the History Channel. I do believe it to be very important to understand just what was the mindset of those who originally placed them there.

I want to show you something on the face of the dollar which you probably have never seen before. Many are unaware of our government's agenda, and what they intend to accomplish. No matter who is in office, they have consistently pushed for one goal, and not so far from now, I'm afraid they will achieve that end. Unfortunately for us, there is a hidden government that is pulling the strings, and we don't elect these powers who hold the true currency of not just the United States, but around the world.

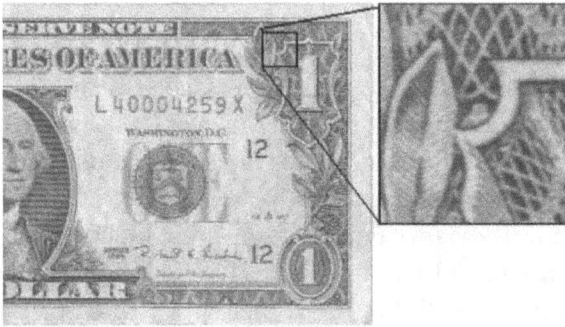

If you look closely at the left-hand corner of the shield in which the 1 is encased, this corner resembles a crescent moon. Perched on this crescent moon is an owl. If you're looking at the above picture, the owl is in the middle of that moon. If you have a magnifying glass at home, you can look at this corner and see it quite clearly on your paper currency. Why is an owl on a dollar bill? I think it's because it is a creature of the night. It is often seen on Halloween decorations, along with witches and skeletons and various items related to evil: creatures of the night, or darkness.

Just below the owl is the seal of the US Treasury, with a mason's square located just below the scales of justice, with 13 stars on the square.

Outside the square, on the shield are 39 stars.

The aforementioned owl can be seen at the Bohemian Grove, s a 2,700-acre campground at 20601 Bohemian Avenue in Monte Rio, CA. In mid-July each year, the Bohemian Club hosts a two-week, three-weekend encampment that is attended by some of the most powerful men in the world

The above picture is from a 1967 meeting. Standing is Harvey Hancock, who was an aviation executive and journalist

who served as the Northern California campaign manager for Richard Nixon's successful 1950 run for the US Senate. To his left is Richard Nixon, and on his right is Ronald Reagan. Also identified in this picture are Glenn T. Seaborg, Jack Sparks, Frank Lindine and Edwin W. Pauley (the gentleman with is back pictured was not identified).

During these meetings, an array of ideas are discussed. During one of the meetings, the atomic bomb was spawned. On the other hand, there is supposedly quite a bit of riotous behavior which I will not disclose as it could possibly be hearsay as I have no documentation.

Going back to this owl, it's a forty-foot hollow steel and concrete owl, identical to the owl pictured on your one-dollar bill. This Owl Shrine is perched at the head of the lake in the grove.

A ceremony is conducted in front of this Owl, the "Cremation of Care," where attendees would be dressed in robes similar to that of the KKK, and have a mock cremation of a figure called "Care."

The attendees of these meetings, past and present were and are, every Republican President since 1888, as well as Fox News CEO, Rupert Murdoch, Warren Buffet, Colin Powell, Donald Rumsfeld, Dick Cheney, Henry Kissinger, Alan Greenspan, John Lehman, Karl Rove, Norman Schwarzkopf, members of the Rockefeller family, e high-ranking members of the ALEC, NATO and NAFTA, Stratfor, Haliburton, The United Nations, Bilderberg Group, CIA, FBI, Federal Reserve, and the 9/11 Report Commission report committee. The list continues to spiral with a laundry list of major players in world politics, big business, the banking industry, and the military industrial complex. I find this a bit scary.

You will not see any news coverage of these seemingly top-secret meetings, or get-togethers. Yet, it is my contention that the top figures of the news media know all about it, and perhaps help cover up these meetings. I will even go so far as to say that even though I cannot find in other sources of the attendees, I believe that these top figures were also in attendance. After all, in past meetings, perhaps in the 60s or 70s, Walter Cronkite himself was the voice of the owl during the cremation ceremony.

Going back to the numbers aspect that this book is about, I want to give you the idea of how I see that time is short, our days are numbered and we should always keep watch as to what's happening. God said in Isaiah 46:10, "Declaring the end *from the beginning, and from ancient times the things that are not done.*"

From this verse, we know that there is going to be an end. After all, we already know there was a beginning. If we go back to the beginning, we see the creation of the world and all that was made in the world. We know that this all came about in six days and on the seventh day God rested. I believe God is showing us a valuable lesson here. Let's look at this. There were six days in the creation. On the seventh day God rested. I believe there is a pattern here, after all there is no new thing under the sun, and God said that that which was done shall be done (Eccl. 1:9).

In 2 Peter 3:8, it says, "***But beloved, be not ignorant of this one thing, that one day is with the Lord as a thousand years, and a thousand years as one day.***" Psalm 90:4 says, "***For a thousand years in thy sight are but as yesterday.***"

In light of the above verses, let's look at the time of creation and count two one thousand-year days and that takes us to Abraham. From Abraham to Jesus takes us another two thousand years for a total of four thousand years, or four days. Jesus to around the year 2000 or the time period which we now live is another two thousand years for a total of six thousand years, the number of days of creation. Some refer to this count as the number of our lease of this world and the one thousand-year reign of Jesus is when our land-Lord rules. That would be our day of rest. If that is so, I would say that our time is short. Jesus should be here on Earth and begin reigning soon. Keep in mind that no man knows the day or hour of His return (Matt. 24:36), but also keep in mind that He left us with a lot of clues to know just about when it would be. He is constantly showing us things almost on a daily basis today. Let' keep our eyes open.

I have a couple more things to address on the one-dollar bill. If you count the number of bricks on the pyramid, there are 72.

Is the number 72 significant to know? Why is it on the dollar? Are we supposed to know the answers to these questions? Is this an important number?

Let's take one last look at the dollar bill for the answers. As you can see, it's full of symbols, none of which resembles our United States. You might say, *how about the American eagle?* With all of the other symbols on this bill, couldn't that eagle actually be the mythical phoenix which fits in with the pyramid? This mythical bird would fit in with the idea of a New World Order, as this bird is supposed to rise out of the ashes, fresh and beautiful, for another long life.

In the occult, numbers mean something, so let's look at this number 72. If we look at the geometry of the Pentagon, all five sides are at a 72-degree angle. According to the Kabbalah (Jewish mysticism), Enoch was transformed into the angel, "Metatron," a 72-winged angel who became godlike or a god. This is what could have spawned a fixation with the number

72. In Saint Peter's Square, surrounding the square there are columns of pillars. Like Metatrons' wings, there are 36 columns on each side for a total of 72.

In Dallas, TX, there is a memorial for JFK. Around the memorial are 72 columns. Inside the US Capitol building, if you look up at artwork on the ceiling at the Apotheosis of Washington you will see a circle of stars with circles around each. These are called *pentagrams*. There just so happens to be 72 of these wrapped around the Apotheosis. Pentagrams are associated with Satan. When a person dies, if he/she isn't cremated they are buried 72 inches below ground. 72 is the normal temperature of a room. 72 is the average number of an adult heartbeat. This list of 72 is quite extensive. As one who likes golf, I wonder why the average par is 72 and why the 18 holes, after all, one can see three sixes in the number 18 or 6-6-6. In championship golf, they play 72 holes. I think this number 72 and 18 in golf is trying to get my mind off my backswing. The human body is 72 percent composed of water. Numbers are what we consist of and what drives us.

As discussed earlier, in the circle where the pyramid is displayed there are exactly 39 letters. I believe the number 39 means something in the scheme of things. In the Bible, where anyone was punished, they would receive 39 lashes. There are 39 books in the Old Testament. So it seems that 39 means something to those that put the symbols on our dollar bill. After all, two important numbers are found in the makeup of 39, which are 13 and 3, as 3 x 13 = 39.

The seals were placed on the one dollar note in 1935, which if added together would come up to 18 or 6 x 3 = 18 or **6+6+6** = 18. The number 3 and 13 carry weight with those involved with numerology.

Genesis 1:14 . . . "And God said, let there be lights in the firmament of the heaven to divide the day from the night; and let them be for signs."

CHAPTER TWO

SIGNS

In this chapter, we will once again look at numbers. As pointed out earlier, our very being has to do with numbers. Numbers are like God. Numbers don't lie, they don't make mistakes, and they're infinite. No matter where you go, what- ever country you're in, 1 + 1 = 2. Numbers are universal, all of today's technology is based on some form of mathematical foundation. Everyone is attached to a number in some way or another, such as a phone or address number, a post box, employee number or some other number not mentioned here. Even if one lives in a tent, you may have a social security number, driver's license number, gun permit number, or a credit card or bank number. You have a birth date, which consists of numbers, so even if you're homeless you can't get away without a number. One number we do not want attached to us is the mark, or number, of the beast. It seems very hard to find someone, no matter where you go, not familiar with the number, 666. If you look in your Bible and turn to Revelation, chapter 13, verse 18 you can read it for yourself.

There are many references to numbers in the Scriptures describing dates, times, hours, et cetera Many of these times are referring to a specific time having to do with the Lord's return and warning to be ready and not being caught off guard. There was a specified time for our Lord's first arrival and there is also a specified time for His soon return. Psalm 90:12, *"Teach us to number our days"* and 2 Corinthians 6:2 says, *"now is the day of salvation."*

We are governed by time; it rules in our lives. We have 60 seconds in a minute, 60 minutes in an hour, 24 hours in a day and 365 days in a year. We have an average of 30 days in a month. If, perhaps, you want to see a dentist, you have to make an appointment. This would mean that at a precise time you will be there taking care of that aching tooth. God made appointments, that ready or not, they will be kept. Heb. 9:27, *"And as it is appointed onto men once to die, but after this the judgment:"* Going back to the beginning, everything is about numbers. Remember, the world was created by or with numbers. God was before numbers. in other words, time was nonexistent. We, in this three-dimensional world are limited to live and work within the constraints of these assigned times. In the Old Testament book of Esther, Queen Esther learned that she was made to be queen to save her people when her uncle told her she was made queen for, *"such a* **time** *as this"* (Est. 4:19). The birth of Jesus was foretold in the book of Genesis, chapter 3, verse 15. In the New Testament book of Gal. 4:4 it says, *"But when the fullness of the time was come, God sent forth his Son, made of a woman, made under the law."*

From these verses we learn that we are governed by

time. We were designed by our Creator to be born in this time period. God lives outside of time; therefore, He has no restraints. He made time and we are limited to its restraints. (Eccl. 3:1-8) Along with time are numbers as discussed earlier. Biblical numbers give us patterns as well as some numbers we find in history. Right now I want to give a brief list of some biblical numbers.

One	First things. unity.
Two	Division or unity, agree as one
Three	Resurrection, number of divinity
Four	Gospel or (fight against) principalities, powers, rulers of darkness in this world, spiritual wickedness in high places.
Five	Grace, redemption
Six	Man
Seven	Completion, perfection.
Eight	New beginnings
Nine	Fruit bearing
Ten	Law
Eleven	Disorder, judgment
Twelve	Government
Thirteen	Rebellion, evil, depravity
Twenty-two	Light, revelation

Forty   Testing, trials

We are all here at a prescribed time to do or be at a place our God had designed us to be. This is our time for Him. Each of us who find work, must work so many hours to receive an hourly income, or earn so much for a salary. You will have numbers involved in your life in some way or another. With the increased technology, it would seem that we are increasingly getting away from paychecks and cash, and becoming more reliant on direct deposit from our employers. And our spending is with credit cards and debit cards, reward cards, insurance cards, et cetera, I would guess that the average person on the street carries no less than six cards. A new card, called the *coin* is in the works. It is supposed to house several of your cards in one. Sounds pretty handy; one card to take care of all your transactions. What if you lose it or someone steals it? Maybe they'll come up with a way to implant it into your skin or something. Kind of makes one wonder. The new Apple phone has this same ability as the coin.

Daniel 12:4, ***"But thou, O Daniel, shut up the words, and seal the book, even to the time of the end: many shall run to and fro, and* knowledge shall be increased."**

There is absolutely no doubt that we, not only as a nation but around the world, are doing things we would never would have believed would be possible. It seems that with today's technology that the world has come up with inventions that ten years ago would have made us say, "That's impossible." Today we have an invisibility cloak that is almost perfected. We have 3D printers, smartphones, smart TVs, holograms with computers that you can carry in your pocket. We also have cars that park themselves, robots that can think. I'm from what many call the old days. I'm still trying to learn how to use the microwave oven.

In these United States we have DARPA, which stands for **D**epartment of **A**dvanced, **R**esearch, **P**roject, **A**gency, which is constantly experimenting on things I cannot even imagine. This program came about when the top scientists from the Nazi regime were removed from Hitler's occupation. After the war they were taken in by our CIA under a program called Operation Paper Clip. That's the same technology which gave Germany the ability to have flying saucers back in the mid 1940s. Today's technology, as far as I know, perfected this type of transportation. As many of the Nazi regime were believed to be Satanist and under occult influences, perhaps their insight was influenced as they received revelation from this source.

According to Scripture, I see that there is a spiritual world that lives outside these constraints. Also, I see that angels, both God's angels and Satan's fallen angels are very active outside our dimension. I found many times that angels appeared to the early patriarchs. I believe that Satan and his angels have been and still are actively busy in most of this supernatural phenomenon observed today.

An example of this are ghosts and UFO's that are discussed on the Science, Discovery and History channels. Many well-known people have observed such phenomena, and most have been reluctant to discuss it. I find that in today's society, however, most people won't laugh them off and dismiss them as some kind of kook. I found in the Scriptures where both ghosts and UFO's seem to be found. The first occurrence of ghost or evil spirits is when King Saul was seeking to summon the prophet Samuel from the dead, so he went to what today is called a fortune-teller. In the Old Testament book of 1 Samuel 28:13 and 14, the fortune-teller is telling Saul what she sees, *"I saw gods ascending out of the earth. And he said unto her, What form is he of? And she said, an old man cometh up; And he was covered with a mantel. And he perceived it was Samuel."* What Saul saw was not Samuel. Saul assumed it was Samuel's ghost, as Samuel was dead. Ghosts are evil spirits. Spirits take on the human form and I believe they can take on almost any other form. Be careful what you pray for.

Now, let's look at UFOs in the Bible. Let me first explain that for many years the most common mode of transportation was the chariot. So if any other mode of transportation came along, they probably would describe it as a chariot. With that in mind let's look at Nahum 2:3 *"the chariots shall be with flaming torches in the day of his preparation."*

It would appear that this verse is talking about our modern mode of transportation Our cars would be around when the Lord is getting ready for His return. With that in mind let's look at 2 Kings 6:17. This was at a time where the king of Syria was trying to capture the prophet of God, Elisha, so they surrounded the city where he was. Elisha's servant stepped out of the house in the morning, and seeing the host of chariots surrounding them, ran into the house in fear telling Elisha of their doom. *"And Elisha prayed, and said, Lord I pray thee, open his eyes that he may see. And the Lord opened the eyes of the young man; and he saw: and behold the mountains was full of horses and chariots of fire round about Elisha."* We see this also in 2 Kings 2:11. I think the Scriptures are speaking of UFOs in Ezekiel's prophecies in chapter 1 and again in chapter 10. Today these flying objects would be called UFOs.

What has all this to do about time? I believe they tell us of the day of our Lord's soon return. Besides, all of the prophets of old and in the New Testament books tell of what we should be looking for. Jesus also left us many things to watch for. Read Matthew 24, Mark 13, and Luke 17 and 21.

Something happened in the middle of the twentieth century that woke up the prophetic time clock and started the prophecy clock to begin once again. Joel 1:7 and Luke 13:6–9 are a few of several Scriptures which refer to a fig tree as a symbol of Israel. Isaiah 66:8, *"Who hath heard such a thing? Who hath seen such a thing? Shall the earth be made to bring forth in one day? or shall a nation be born at once? for as soon as Zion travailed, she brought forth her children."* Israel is at the center of time. Matthew 24:32, 33 says, *"Now learn a parable of the fig tree; When his branch is yet tender, and putteth forth leaves, ye know that summer is nigh: So Likewise ye, when ye shall see all these things, know that it is near, even at the door."*

The aforementioned verses have to do with the end times, or should I say the times in which we are living in today? On May 14, 1948, the date that the nation of Israel was born, President Truman was the first national leader to congratulate Israel and recognize them as a nation. Once Israel was restored, with that, God returned to them the Hebrew language which was unspoken for over a thousand years. (Zeph. 3:9) I think we have been blessed as a nation because of our support of Israel. Genesis 12:3, *"And I will bless them that bless thee, and curse them that curseth thee."*

Today our nation has become a dictator over the nation of Israel. We tell them that they have no right to build in Jerusalem and to split part of their land with the Palestinians.

As part of a peace plan, initiated by the US and Palestine, Israel gave them the Gaza strip, which Hamas then used to launch rockets into Israel. The tiny nation of Israel has been and will always be the focal point of the world. I believe all the woes of our nation today mostly have to do with us turning our back on Israel.

If there are any other doubts about God's hand over Israel, we should consider the war for Jerusalem in 1967. Jordan, Egypt, and Syria decided they should overrun Israel and take Jerusalem. They outnumbered the Israel forces by three to one and their military weaponry was even greater. Not only did they not win this war, but the combined forces lost the war in six days. Psalm 122:6 tells us to pray for the peace of Jerusalem.

I would like to discuss some moral issues that our country is facing today. Over a period of time it seems our hearts as a nation have darkened and become hard hearted. Before I continue, I would like to say that these issues which I will be discussing have to do with time and prophecy. First, I would like to mention abortions. We talk of the child in the womb as a fetus, nothing more than a piece of tissue. Not so fast, this fetus is a living organism, a separate life living inside the womb. When Mary, the mother of Jesus, mentioned she was pregnant to her cousin Elizabeth, who was six months pregnant with John the Baptist, the baby in her womb heard the news and jumped. Read Psalm 139:13 and Isaiah 66:8 through 16. Unfortunately, we are not the first to kill our children. Leviticus 18:21, ***"And thou shall not let any of thy seed pass through the fire to Molech."*** What they were doing at the time was throwing their living children into a fire to sacrifice them to a god named Molech. Pretty much what we are doing with the abortion clients today as children are being ripped from their mothers' wombs limb by limb. As of this date we have aborted a total of 55 million babies.

Another issue I would like to address is sodomy. This is immorality, not a civil rights issue, and should not be addressed as anything else. We, as Christians, do not hate these people or wish to suppress their rights. We do not approve of their actions or morals. We should not have this issue paraded before us or be forced to accept this behavior. We would like them to understand that God loves them, but not their sins, just as He loves us and not our sins.

Christians, like any other people in this world, are not without sin. The difference is we do not wish to continue in our sins and try to, with God's help, not sin. We do not go forth with the same mindset as to continue to walk in the lust of the flesh. I think we are under attack, an all-out, war with Satan in these last days and should try to understand who our enemy is. If you look at Genesis 19, you can see what the days of Lot were like. The Bible tells us that the same will happen at the last days. Read Luke 17:28, 29.

If by any chance you fell into this perverted lifestyle, you can be changed. I think, I do not know for sure, there are what's known as a chemical imbalance in many people and many have been treated. Before I conclude with this topic, yes David loved Jonathan, just as I love my brother and would never consider to partake in an immoral act. Please don't shut me off and slam this book down without considering what this book is about. "Time is short."

This is about time, and time is happening in a biblical sense in a big way. This is that day our Lord warned us about. Today, with our technology we are doing everything we can to prolong our lives, to become the very thing that Satan told Eve in the Garden of Eden when he said, "You shall be as gods." We're trying to stretch out the human life. We're having tummy tucks, face lifts, implants and only God and DARPA know what else.

Something else is happening in Geneva, Switzerland, which perhaps you may not be aware of: the experiments with the Large Hadron Collider. This is an underground project which cost the United States alone $531 million for the development and components for the LHC, with the US Department of Energy shelling out $450 million and the National Science Foundation kicking in the remaining $81 million. Almost every major country in the world has joined in with the support of this project.

This collider is called CERN. In 1952 European countries came together to form the European Council for Nuclear Research (*Conseil European pour la Rechereche Nucleaire* in French, which gave it the acronym CERN). If CERN sounds familiar to you before you ever heard of it, that's because the World Wide Web was started by CERN employees, Sir Tim Berners-Lee and Robert Cailliau.

A collider is a type of a particle accelerator with directed beams of particles traveling in opposite directions and colliding at a certain point. In particle physics, colliders are used as a research tool: they accelerate particles to very high kinetic energies and let them impact other particles. With these experiments, the physicists hope they will answer some of the fundamental questions in physics concerning the basic laws governing the interactions and forces among the elementary objects, the deep structure of space and time, and in particular the interrelation between quantum mechanics and general relativity, where current theories and knowledge are unclear or break down altogether. I don't comprehend these things as I relate them with you, as I don't understand the physics behind them. I do understand some of the concepts behind what they are trying to achieve, such as space and time and what are the properties of quark-gluon. These, I believe, are answered in the Scriptures. I am bringing up the whole concept of the collider because I think I found these questions are addressed in the Bible.

As I have mentioned, the Large Hadron Collider is in Geneva, Switzerland. What else is made in Switzerland that comes to mind besides chocolate? I hope you thought of watches. That's also what I thought. The LHC is a 17-mile circular tunnel ranging from 164 to 574 feet underground. The concrete-lined tunnel was constructed between 1983 to 1989, and was formerly used to house the Collider. It crosses the border between Switzerland and France at four points, with most of it in France. The Collider tunnel contains two adjacent parallel beam line pipes that intersect at four points, each containing a proton beam, which travel just under the speed of light in opposite directions, and to my understanding just broke the speed of light.

Relating this Collider with a watch is the fact that not only is this smashing particles, trying to create the God Particle, or what holds them together, but they are looking at time travel. At this time, two of the physicists working at the Collider site, Tom Weller and Chui Man Ho, believe they're close to the knowledge of sending matter back in time. "Our theory is a long shot," admitted Weller, who is a physics professor at Vanderbilt University, "but it doesn't violate any laws of physics or experiment constraints."

I disagree with their findings, I am not saying that this

could not be possible, what I am saying is that God created time in the beginning. I believe if it is possible for anything having to do with time travel being achieved, that God would intervene. Jesus Christ first came here   on Earth, at the fullness of time, according to Gal. 4:4, which says, "*But when the fullness of time was come, God sent forth his Son.*" I believe the same for His soon return. He gave us things to watch for, showing us just how close we are to His soon return.

There is so much more to say about the LHC, most of which I really can't grab ahold of as I am not a physicist. The only thing I could put down on paper at this point is what I found in Wikipedia and other resources found on the internet.

What I have to say regarding this topic from here is how I thought the Scriptures seem to have already addressed it. Let us go all the way back to the first book in the Bible.

We're looking at Genesis 11. This event in chapter 11 occurs about two hundred years after the flood. I believe this is just after or maybe at the time of the building of the ancient pyramids and other similar structures that have been found around the world. These people were no dummies who would grunt at each other while scratching their heads and sleeping in caves. They had a king named Nimrod who was evil. What got my attention was in this chapter they were building a city and a tower (the Tower of Babel). What's unique about this tower is the people who were building it said, speaking of the tower, "***whose top may reach unto heaven.***" We automatically think of a structure higher than any structure that has been built today.

How could these master builders make such a statement that a physical tower will reach up to heaven? I don't think this structure had so much to do with the height. I think it may have been possible that these people who had come together may have had the knowledge of building a portal to another dimension or time travel, such as CERN today.

In chapter 11, the first 9 verses have to do with the people and tower. After verse 9 there is no more mention of these people who were divided over the face of Earth, and no more mention of the tower. What I found even more interesting in this chapter is verse 6, which says, **"And the Lord said, Behold, the people is one, and they have all one language; and this they begun to do: and now nothing will be restrained from them, *which they have imagined to do.*"**

Did you see that? *"Nothing will be restrained from them."* Isn't this saying that they could have built some kind of portal or stargate reaching into heaven? In light of this verse, I think it is something to consider. I don't think these great builders would think for a minute that a structure could possibly reach into the outer atmosphere. I think it is also interesting that chapter 11 verse 9 is the last we hear that has to do with the tower. I think that it is important. Keep that thought. I will address this in another chapter.

I think there might be a link between what happened then with this tower and what's happening today with this Collider. I think we might be opening a portal, perhaps to another dimension. This is just a thought; I have not found anything to substantiate this statement. I have heard that the first day they started the Collider, in September of 2008, there were several small earthquakes and UFO sightings that were reported. There are many other experiments happening around the world that we have absolutely no idea of what's going on.

I know that there are many conspiracy theories going around, not just what I brought up with the Collider, but with others such as things like HAARP. The HAARP is an acronym for High Frequency Active Auroral Research Program. I'm still not sure if some of these theories are just theories, but may be the cause of such things as the unexplained number of birds dropping dead while in flight with no explanation or the number of sea creatures washing up on shores around the world. This could also possibly have something to do with the strange weather patterns with the long cold winters, the inordinate amount of flooding with the heavy rains and maybe with the amount of sink holes opening all around the world. This makes me think of Rev. 9:2–3, *"And he opened the bottomless pit; as the smoke of a great furnace; and the sun and the air were darkened by reason of the smoke of the pit. And there came out of the smoke locust upon the earth: and unto them was given power, as the scorpions of the earth have power."*

Over the years I have developed a distrust with the decisions of our government. I learned of the Club of Rome, the CFR. the Trilateral Commission, the Bilderberg Group, the Illuminati and many more secret societies, like the Skull and Bone Society that have their agendas. One of the big things that happened in the twentieth century was when President Woodrow Wilson allowed the existence or the birth of the Federal Reserve System, which is not at all Federal, but private bankers getting rich while making many of us poor by devaluating our dollar. I believe that the whole concept behind that is to bring us to a one-world monitory system.

Revelation 13:16–18. *"And he causeth all, both small and great, rich and poor, free and bond, to receive a mark in their right hand or in their foreheads: And that no man may buy or sell, save he that had the mark, or the name of the beast, or the number of his name. Here is wisdom. Let him that hath understanding count the number the number of the beast; for it is the number of a man; and his number is Six hundred threescore and six."*

Genesis 6:14 . . . "Make thee an ark of gopher wood; The length of the shall be three hundred cubits, the breadth of it fifty cubits, and the height of it thirty cubits."

CHAPTER THREE

HIDDEN NUMBERS IN STRUCTURES

Throughout the Scriptures, numbers are given by God pointing out specific measurements of either land or objects that were built. Some examples are the size of Noah's ark, the ark of the covenant, Solomon's temple to worship God or even the dimensions of Israel's Promised Land, all mentioned in the Old Testament right up to the New Testament and into the book of Revelation and the New Jerusalem which will come down from heaven. All the numbers dimensions given by God have special meaning. I believe the same is true with measurements and numbers used by man. I will point this out with recent structures that have been built over the last couple hundred years and some a lot less.

The inspiration of this chapter comes from a documentary I came across several years ago by Adullam Films entitled *Riddles in Stone*. Since that time, I started to take a closer look at what was going on and just what was being built. The most recent discovery thing that I came across had been built some time ago, was an unfinished pyramid in North Dakota in Cavalier County, much like what is found on the reverse of the one-dollar bill.

The above structure is called the Stanley R Mickelsen Safeguard Complex. As you can see, it is complete with the All-Seeing Eye. The eye is also looking in all four directions. This pyramid was built as an anti-ballistic missile complex in the early 70s, at the height of Cold War. The military installation that houses this structure was once the site's control building, and was used to detect a potential Soviet nuclear attack. The circular eyes were actually radars scanning the horizon for inbound missiles. The site was named after a retired US. Lt. General who was a former commanding general of the US Army Defense whose insight brought us from bullets to missiles.

This site was completed and went into operation on

October 1, 1975 and was decommissioned October 2, 1975. Congress ended the safeguard program and deactivated the site. Since then, the hundred-plus underground missiles were removed and the pyramid was sealed. In 2012, the facility was bought by the Spring Creek Hutterite Colony for $530,000. Although they purchased the property, the US government requires that this group has no rights to make any changes to the property. This site sits on the 99th meridian, which I find interesting. That would be 33 x 3 = 99. The number 33 has been used in numerology, as well as the number 3. If one goes to the website gizmodo.com and reads the very first sentence, a portion, speaking of the pyramid says "tracking the end of the world." There remain several mysteries to this day surrounding this pyramid, such as why this structure is still standing. Why can't the new owners of this property make any changes on their own property? Why the pyramid? I think the list of questions could continue. The answers are probably buried at Area 51. This structure is one of the most recent I could find that I believe has hidden meanings.

Washington, DC, is an entire city that has hidden meaning, which much has been revealed by way of recent technology and a great deal of research by some brilliant people. One such person is the creator of Adullam Films. In their documentary entitled *Riddles in Stone*, you see an overview of the streets of Washington, DC, and the patterns that are found. Anyone who sees these things should know that the layout of the streets and the structures that were built did not come out the way they did by accident. The symbols and number patterns had to have been planned by the architects who designed them.

Let's start by looking at just one pattern found in the

street lay

Looking at the above, one can see clearly there is pentagram encased inside a pentagon in the street layout of streets of DC. There is much controversy on this topic. I think one should do a little of their own research to draw their own conclusion. The pentagram points or stops at the White house.

The next structure I would like to point out is the obelisk or better known as the Washington Monument. This is the world's tallest obelisk, standing 555 feet 5 1/2 inches tall.

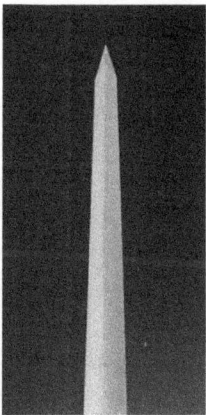

At the time of its completion, the monument was the world's tallest building. Today it stands as the world's tallest stone structure. Converting the entire measurements to inches, it is **6,666** inches tall, and from corner to corner is **666** inches square. I don't think this happened by accident. This monument is in some circles known as Baal's Shaft or male organ of Osiris. Like the street layout this is also a highly debated topic, like most of the other structures in our nation's capital.

The capstone that forms a pyramid on top of the obelisk weighs exactly 3,300 pounds; again, 33 being a master number in numerology. These double numbers will be discussed in the chapter "Numerology." The number 72 is also important. In that the kabbalah, the power of God can be invoked by pronouncing the 72 names of God, each comprised of a combination of three of the twenty-two Hebrew letters. It just so happens that the Washington Monument was dedicated on July 4, 1848, or exactly 72 years from our Independence Day. Inside the obelisk is a spiral staircase that just so happens to be 33 stories tall.

While on the topic of the obelisk, it just so happens that our monument and capitol building in DC are almost a mirror image of that in Saint Peter's Square in Rome. The obelisk in the Vatican was transferred there from ancient Heliopolis, the city of "On" in the Bible. dedicated to Ra, Osiris, and Isis, according to Tom Horn's book, *Apollyon Rising*.

The Lincoln Memorial was commissioned by an act of Congress in 1910 and was designed to reflect one of the Seven Wonders of the World, the ancient Temple of Zeus in Athens. In other words, it was designed as a temple. The true meaning is a false god is in the seat of authority. Inside the Lincoln Memorial you have a statue of Lincoln, made to resemble the statue of Zeus, the god of thunder. He is seated on a seat not reserved for a president but for a god-king. Lincoln was assassinated by a head wound. Well, we find in Rev. 13:3, ***"And I saw one of his heads as it was wounded to death; and his deadly wound was healed and all the world wondered after the beast."*** If you look at the Memorial you will find that it has ten interior columns. Each one of these columns is 50 feet tall and 5 feet 6 inches wide at the base. When the length and width of these columns is converted into inches, we see that their height comes to 600 inches and their width is precisely 66 inches. Wouldn't you know it; the number comes out to be **666**. I would like to mention that the outer structure of the memorial is 99 feet tall. This number is a numerology expression of the number 33 (33 x 3), a number associated with the beast who rises from the lower depths of the sea.

I found an article written by William Henry, (williamhenry.net) entitled, "The US Capitol and the Temple in Man." In this article he writes,

> *The United States Capitol, rising atop Capitol Hill in the monument city of Washington, DC, may well be the most famous building in the world. To Americans the cast-iron, Capitol dome, dressed in pure white sandstone, is a symbol of strength and democracy. Radiant, luminous, shining, freedom rings from this beautiful bell. How many recognize that the Capitol is a temple? Thomas Jefferson called it "The first temple dedicated to the sovereignty of the people."*

> *The dome of the Capitol ices this connection. Domes have been called the perfect architectural shape: the circle, symbol of the universe, executed in three dimensions. In religious architecture, domes proclaim the glory of God. The word dome comes from Latin domus, meaning a house, via Italian duomo, a house of God that is a church. The temple is a "house of the holy." Temple is also a word for the flat part on either side of the human head, called a dome in slang, above and beyond the eye. The oculus*

or the eye of the dome is considered the Gateway of the Sun. From this gateway at the top of the dome rises the World Axis. The link between heaven and earth. Domes, therefore, are the threshold or gateway of the spiritual world.

This was all taken from the article of William Henry, and you can probably guess from the closing of this article I don't agree with him on all that he says, while I did find it to be most interesting.

One of the seven ancient wonders of the world was the Colossus of Rhodes. It was described as a giant statue, some 109 feet tall, made of brass. It was a depiction of Helios, the Greek sun god, worshipped all over the world in many ways and under many names, including Osiris. The statue featured Helios adorned with a halo consisting of 7 rays, another reference to the 7 spirits of the antichrist. I find it hard not to think of this statue without having a picture of the Statue of Liberty come into mind. It is in fact a feminized copy of the Colossus of Rhodes, including the 7 rays extending from her corona, or halo.

I find it interesting that at the base of our statue is an inscription which reads in part, "Give me your tired, your poor, your huddled masses yearning to breathe," written by Emma Lazarus in 1883, and engraved on a plaque at the base of the statue in 1903. The poem's title is "The New Colossus.". The interior design of the Statue features a winding staircase (DNA) that leads the visitor on an upward journey to the 7 rays of illumination. The base upon which it stands was built in the shape of an 11-pointed star; 11 being a symbol of the unfinished work at the Tower of Babel.

The next structure I want to introduce is an aircraft carrier, but before I do, I need to lay out some information on how I found the date of the topic to be relevant. Everyone is well aware of our Independence Day and the year 1776. Something else happened just before July 1. On May 1, 1776, Adam Wieshaupt formed the Illuminati. This date is significant, as it turns out this is the 121st day of the year that happens to be 11 x 11. This would then connect the formation of Weishaupt's Illuminati with not only the rise of the beast from the bottomless pit, but also with the transhuman efforts of mankind in the story of the Tower of Babel in Genesis 11. The rebuilt remains of ancient Babylon, where the tower of Babel was built, are located in Iraq, just south of the capital city of Baghdad. The city is positioned at roughly 33 degrees north latitude and 44 degrees east longitude. When added together these two numbers equal the magical occult number 77.

With the aforementioned numbers and date given I can now address the aircraft carrier, the USS *Abraham Lincoln*. It was on May 1, 2003 (the 121st day of the year) that President George W Bush, flew to this aircraft carrier on his way back to port San Diego, CA, to deliver his now famous "Mission Accomplished" speech—even though we were still there with our troops.

This navel carrier that was selected had the navel designation of CVN-72. If you look at the letters as numbers with *C* being the 3rd number in the alphabet and so on, the letters would add up to 39. It so happens we have two seals on the one-dollar bill. On the face we have the treasury seal. Inside this you will find a masons square with 13 stars on it. Outside the mason square and in the circle are 39 stars. On the reverse side where the pyramid is located you will find inside that circle 39 letters. There are 39 books in the Old Testament. Anytime anyone was beaten, they would receive 40 stripes, save one. In other words, they received 39 lashes. That's 40 minus one. From our previous paragraph we learned the significance of the number 72. What also is interesting is that on October 7, 2006 naval carrier CNV-77 was named the *George H. W. Bush,* after the father of George W. Bush.

A couple of paragraphs referring to the Lincoln Memorial and the Colossus came from Pastor Mike Hoggards' book, *Capital Secrets.*

Psalms 71:15 . . . "My mouth shall show forth thy righteousness and thy salvation all the day: for I know not the numbers thereof."

CHAPTER FOUR

NUMBERS AND THE BIBLE

In the opening I have a passage from Psalm 71 illustrating that we don't know the number of our days. Psalm 90:12 says we should ask God to teach us to number our days. Going back to Psalm 71:15 we find the word *numbers*. Because we will be discussing the importance of numbers, I wanted to open with the word *numbers* and show the significance of not just the meaning of the word, but so often how many times certain words are used in the Bible. They seem to point to what I think God wants us to know. That is to say they seem to point to a particular theme.

Please bear with me as I try to explain. For instance, the word "numbers", is only 3 times in the entire bible. What does the number three bring to your mind? If you thought of the Godhead, your right. Think about this: numbers don't lie. Couldn't this also be used to describe God? It does coincide with the thought. It also points to man as a three-part being, 1 Thessalonians 5:23. Numbers seem to speak to us.

When God created the world, one of the first things that you notice is God numbering the days. Numbers are important. Secondly, you can see that those numbers make a separation of the days of creation, and lay out the pattern of our weeks. It's also important to see just what was created on each of those days and just what was assigned to be created on the number of that day. Looking at the days of creation, they always end with the evening and the morning before the next day is created. What I found interesting, as most of you probably did as well, was we had the evening and morning before the fourth day when the sun and moon were created. In this fourth day of creation, verse 1:14 says that the lights were given to divide the day from the night and that they were for 1) signs, 2) seasons, 3) days, and 4) years, this is important to ponder.

Could the prediction by NASA of the four blood moon tetrad, which all appear on Jewish feast days this year and next have anything to do with those signs?

The 4 blood moons first appear on 4/15/14, then again on 10/8/14, again on 4/4/15 and concluded on 9/28/15). I will discuss this phenomenon again with a little more detail in chapter 7, "Events and Dates Possibly Revealing End Times." We can also look at weather patterns, which are given as signs as mentioned in Matthew 24 and also in Luke 21:25, as it mentions the sea and the waves roaring, men's hearts failing them for fear. We have seen many of these activities in our times, such as the recent tsunamis.

Continuing with the days of creation, the seventh day does not mention the evening and morning because creation of all that is around us, plants animal and human life was complete. The numbered days were set apart to show us a pattern for our week. There is, however, this thought: this seventh day is left open for those who are being made new creations in Him, as described in 2 Corinthians 5:17. Think about that when you worship on your Sabbath. Before we leave Genesis 1, notice man is made on the sixth day of creation; therefore, the number of man is six. Today, mankind lives on six continents and there is no written history of man found beyond 6,000 years. As it turns out, in this day our modern scientists understand from the periodic table of chemical elements that man is made up of mainly carbon; and its atomic number, wouldn't you know, is 6. Antarctica is the only continent not yet suitable for long-term survival of man, accounting for the 6 continents on which man resides. The numbers God uses seem almost to predict things that are still hidden from man. We will look more closely at numbers as we continue.

The Bible that we have today is most convenient, as we don't have to search through ancient scrolls written in three different languages. Compare this also to the easy-to-read chapters and verses. Imagine trying to find a specific quote or a specific word or thought in those scrolls. The chapters came about in the twelfth century by Stephen Langton. The verses didn't become widely popular until 1551 by the work of Robert Estienne. Even though these two individuals were not part of the holy men of God (2 Peter 1:21) who penned His Word, I do believe that their work was inspired by God.

Predictions and prophecy themes have been written for hundreds of years and still are being written today, as this book could be considered to be just one of the many. I can assure you that this is not such a book, but a book mostly of facts that may seem to point to prophecy. Before I continue,

I must say that I did inject a few thoughts I had along the way. I can't tell you of the number of these books predicting a big-time event that have turned out to be nothing more than what a person thought might happen and have turned out to be nothing. For instance, there are books being sold today on the tetrad blood moons at your local Christian book stores at the time of this writing.

There is one book on prophecy that came along in the twelfth century which was supposedly written by Archbishop Malachy entitled *Prophecies of the Popes*. This writing contained a list of all the popes from the twelfth century, where he started with the first pope and concludes with the 112th pope who sits in this office today and is said, according to this prophecy, is to be the one that ushers in the Antichrist. At the time of this writing, our current pope is now 76 years old, born on December 17, 1936. Maybe we won't have to wait that long to see if this prophecy (or should I say prediction) is true. Before I continue. I must say there is only one good and perfectly accurate true word of prophecy, and that is the Holy Bible. There is, however, one book that caught my eye on this pope prophecy topic entitled *The Final Pope Is Here Petrus Romanus*. This book was written and in my hands well before the 112th pope stepped into office. In it, the authors stated that the 111th pope will step down, ushering in the 112th pope. The authors are Thomas Horn and Cris Putnam. It's just shy of 500 pages. Don't let that intimodate you. It keeps your interest; making it easy to read. The authors, who stated that the current pope would step down, seemed to know what they were talking about. The 111th pope did step down, vacating his office for the 112th pope. The last pope to step down from this office was roughly 800 years ago. I did find a couple of scriptures in the Bible that seemly give credence to this prophecy.

The first, which I believe you may be aware of, is found in Luke 10:18, speaking of Satan falling as lightning. After Pope Benedict XVI announced that he was stepping down and the day before the 112th pope was announced, lightning struck St Peter's Basilica, ushering in the 112th pope. The second verse I found is in the book of Hosea. This verse was in chapter 13 of this book, which closely follows Revelation 13, both describing the beast. In Hosea 13:3 we find a description of those who have fallen into sin and pass on. What really caught my attention, was that in this verse it mentions the smoke out of the chimney? On March 13 we had the smoke out of the chimney ushering in the 112th pope; the smoke from the chimney found in the 13th chapter, the third verse, or 13th day, 3rd month. I wonder: Is this just a coincidence or something more? This is the only mention of a chimney found in the Bible.

I had never given any thought to the importance of numbers and counting of things until I came across the teachings of Pastor Mike Hoggard. I will be using much of his teaching from this point on to lay the groundwork to what I have learned. I believe what I found could possibly be yet another sign of the nearness of our Lord's return. Keep in mind that this is just my thought or my own opinion. Through numbers, I have found that they lay out patterns in most everything, and, therefore, I will show you the pattern that I stumbled upon through the teachings of Pastor Hoggard. I must reiterate that this is nothing more than a pattern and not an end-time prophecy. I found that it is just something to consider. Through God's word we can find sure signs to watch for, thereby we can know that we are surely in the last days.

If you would like to read Pastor Hoggard's teachings. you can receive them by either going to his webpage at visitbethelchurch.com or by writing to Pastor Michael Hoggard, Prophetic Research Ministry, 1233 American Legion Dr., Festus, MO. 63028.

Portions of the following will be inserts by Pastor Mike, mixed in with my thoughts and opinions from what I have learned. The next chapter was contributed by Pastor Mike. This teaching is the basic one that inspired this book. I hope you will get the same "wow" factor that I did.

Going back to creation, let's go to the book of Colossians 1:16 where we find this to be speaking of Christ, *"FOR BY HIM WERE ALL THINGS CREATED, THAT ARE IN HEAVEN, AND THAT ARE IN EARTH. VISIBLE AND INVISIBLE, WHETHER THEY BE THRONES, OR DOMINIONS, OR PRINCIPALITIES, OR POWERS: ALL THINGS WERE CREATED BY HIM AND FOR HIM."*

We can see by this verse that everything (and that means everything) the entire universe was created by Him and for Him, His pleasure.

I know that when I look at the sky, the stars, moon, trees, I find God's creation most awesome. There have been many paintings and/or photographs and even the Hubble telescope capturing the beauty of God's creation. With the Hubble Telescope we have the ability to look closely at what once was thought to be a single star that is actually galaxies which consist of a galaxy cluster with billions upon billions of stars in each and every one of them. To think we are looking at only at a small amount of our universe. If we break the word *universe* we get "one verse." This is what we have in our Bible, verses

NUMBERS AND THE BIBLE

of Scripture. The word *universe* literally means everything turning into one or united as they turn into one. As you look at the galaxy, you see it as a spiral of stars that appear to be spinning into one. That is what the entire universe looks like and all was created by our God.

Think about this: 2 Peter 3:5 says, *"For this they willingly are ignorant of, that by the word of God, the heavens were of old, and the earth standing out of the water, and in the water."* In other words, the Bible is specifically saying to us that God created the entire universe by speaking to them, by saying, I want this done. In these galaxy spirals we find a pattern that is pretty much what all of creation has in common.

Back in the eleventh century there was a mathematician named Fibonacci. He wrote a book, and in this book he identified a pattern of numbers that he could find in a lot of places. You know this pattern today as the Fibonacci sequence. It goes like this: If you add one to zero, you would get one. If we take then that number one and add it to the previous number one, we get the next number in sequence which is two. If we add two plus one we get three, if we add three plus two, that's five, five plus three is eight, eight plus five is thirteen, plus eight is 21, and the sequence continues, 21, 34, 55, 89, 144, 233, 377, 610, 987, and it can go on.

As the numbers go higher, Fibonacci found that he actually had what's called a ratio. The ratio of the Fibonacci sequence is 1 to 1.618. If you were to take the number 610 and 987, you'll find that 987 is approximately 1.618 times 610. It's called the Fibonacci sequence, or the Golden Ratio, or God's ratio. Fibonacci found that if you take these numbers, this sequence, and lay them   in blocks portioned to the size of the numbers, you would or could create a spiral, ending up with what's known as the Fibonacci spiral.

This teaching is found in greater detail in Pastor Mikes' DVD teaching showing pictures and all the details of this spiral that is revealed in God's creation. I will try to explain, giving some word pictures of the examples of these creations. One common example is the simple sea shell that starts in a tight circle and expands outward. Another would be a ram's horn. Or have you ever looked at a sink full of water when you pull the plug as the water spins in a spiral fashion and appears to spin faster at the base where the spiral gets tighter at the drain? This spiral is found in nearly all creation, from the galaxies to weather fronts such as hurricanes, tornadoes to so much more. So we can clearly see Gods' mathematics right before our eyes. It's explained this way in Gods' Word in 1 John. 1:1, *"That which was from the beginning, which we have heard, which we have seen with our eyes, which we have looked upon, and our hands have handled, of the Word of life."* This same spiral is found in man.

Leaving this topic for a moment, I want you to know what I'm going to show you in the upcoming chapters. They are not all necessarily biblical, as they are not found in the Holy Scriptures, but the Scriptures seem to allude to it.

Our Bible shows signs such as the increasing number of earthquakes, the tsunamis, the wars, rumors of wars, the persecution of Christian believers, and knowledge being increased at an explosive rate. We also know through the Scriptures that our current monetary system will soon fail. This will lead to receiving a mark in our right hand or forehead, a method, perhaps, of not only making a purchase, but some type of GPS device. The technology is there. Christians were warned to watch for the blood moon tetrad. Blood moons are mentioned in Joel 2:31 and Acts 2:20, but the tetrad doesn't account for the prophetic sign of the stars not shining and the skies being dark.

You remember the Y2K scare don't you? Many churches jumped on that bandwagon and were preaching gloom and doom. The church that I was attending at the time was stocking up on canned goods and selling generators in the vestibule of the church. They were also inviting secular money advisors to stand behind the pulpit advising the church how to handle their financial status. Where was God in this?

These kind of writings and preaching of gloom and doom, these teaching seems to discredit the Christian. Afterward they hurt us insofar as making us (Christians) look like kooks. Don't sell the farm. We as Christians should always be sharing God's Word. There are plenty of signs in the Scriptures found in Matthew, Mark, and Luke, just to name a few, that tell us we're on short time. When these "prophets" come out with the day and/or time of our 'ord's return that may seem to fall in line to what the scriptures describe as to what will happen, they seem to discredit God's Word. That's because they didn't actually come from His word. That is why these things they prophesized or predicted never materialized. Remember, 1 Peter 1:19, "*We have also a more sure word of prophecy.*"

We (Christians) have the tendency to take things that are happening that seem to give the appearance of lining up with these predictions, such as Y2K that we discussed, and thus making our own time frame for our Lord's return. There are a few things at the time that seem to be earth-shaking. Even without this book and books like it, we can open our Bible and can say, "Wow, it's happening just the way God said it would." I do believe, however, God equipped us with His Word for this purpose, and in doing so, we can see many things happening in our time that are showing us it won't be long before He returns. I also believe God is showing us certain things that fall in line with what's happening and just how close we are to the end of the world as we know it. That is what this book is all about. So please ponder what you are reading and consider the source.

Read your Bible; wait on the Lord. I do believe that God uses each and every one of us to speak hope and inspiration to others. The purpose of this writing is to motivate us to study His Word. But, like you, I am just a normal human (at least I would like to think I am). I believe God is showing His children things so we can get motivated and inspired about reaching out to others and bring them into the sheep fold. He's coming soon!

The next chapter will basically be Pastor Michael Hoggard's teaching on the subject of the temple of God relating it to mankind and what he found in his studies and what I learned through his studies. I hope you will learn what he discovered and it will inspire you as it did me. This teaching made me appreciate my Bible so much more, insofar as realizing I had an accurate translation of the Bible. And as I said before, I learned to count things as a result of this teaching. I believe after this teaching you will find that it matters which Bible you have.

I found that the King James Bible to be a most sure word and most reliable. All Scripture references in this book are from the KJV Bible. I will share a brief history of the KJV Bible at this time. It was translated from the original languages in 1611 by 54 translators who collaborated with each other over seven years. Most of the modern translations, if not all, do not come from the original language, and if they do, it may be by one or just a couple translators, who many have formed their own opinions of what they think the word that they are translating means. I will give you a couple of examples; The NIV translation says in 2 Timothy 2:15, "Do your best to present yourself to God as one approved, a worker who does not need to be ashamed and who correctly handles the word of truth." Whereas the King James says, *"Study to show thyself approved unto God, a workman that needeth not to be ashamed, rightly dividing the word of truth."*

The NIV tells us to do our best. Doing your best is what you have been trying to do all of your life, and have always fallen short. In the KJV, it tells us to study His Word and follow after Him and we will know what to do. There are over 10,000 fewer words in most of our modern translations. Rev. 1:5 is another example. Many of these modern bibles have changed "washed" us from our sins to "loosed" us or "freed" us. In the KJV, that *sin* is nowhere to be found, you've been cleaned, and you're washed in the blood. If you have been loosed from prison or set free, you will still have that record following you around, but if it's been washed away, it's no longer found. I believe that with over two hundred translations it is not surprising that we find so many different types of churches. People today just don't know what to believe.

I have two more verses for comparison I would like to show you from the KJV and the NIV. First I will show you the two verses from the KJV. The first is from 2 Peter 1:19. *"We have also a more sure word of prophecy; whereunto ye do well that ye take heed, as unto a light that shineth in a dark place, until the day dawn, and the day star arise in your hearts:*"

Now, the same verse from the NIV. **"We also have the prophetic message as something completely reliable, and you will do well to pay attention to it, until the day dawns and the** morning star_**rises in your hearts**" (emphasis mine). Did you see the difference between the two? If not, I will give just one more verse from both books showing you just what I want to point out.

The next is from Isaiah 14:12, KJV. "*How art thou fallen from heaven, O Lucifer, son of the morning! how art thou cut down to the ground, which didst weaken the nations!*"

Now, the same from the NIV. **"How you have fallen from heaven,** morning star, **son of the dawn! You have been cast down to the earth, you have once laid low the nations!**" (emphasis mine) Looking at these two verses from the KJV, you see that these are entirely different, talking about two separate issues. Look carefully at "morning star," this term is supposed to describe Jesus. KJV Rev. 2:28 and 22:16. Looking at the NIV, these two verses can cause confusion insofar as 2nd Peter tells you that the morning star rises in your heart and in Isaiah that the morning star is Satan.

The King James Bible was actually used as a textbook for the children back in the mid-seventeenth and eighteenth century when the pilgrims settled here. It really isn't that hard to understand. We look at our country today and wonder what's wrong with our children today. Maybe it's because, in our schools today they don't allow Bibles or prayer in schools. I heard it's because it's harmful to our children, or it might offend another child who is taught at home that there is no God. And today there are other children who have a different god and if you bring a Bible you also have to have a Qu'ran.

At one time, if you came to this country you would have to believe the way this country was and its Christian principles or leave or just keep quiet. You would also have to learn our language. Today if you come to this country, you just believe the way you want and if we don't believe that way, we have to shut up and stop believing the way we want in public. It seems it's against the law to pray in Jesus name, pray and/or read the Bible on government property. These type of things seem also to support just how close we are to our Lord's return. I guess we should just keep looking up. After all, one of these times he will be there.

On December 8, 2008, Cynthia McFadden of ABC news interviewed President George W. Bush. when the topic switched to the Bible, the interviewed went as follows;

McFadden: "Is it literally true, the Bible?"

Bush: "You know. Probably not . . . . No, I'm not a literalist, but I think you can learn a lot from it, but I do think that the New Testament for example is . . . has got . . . . You know, the important lesson is God sent a son."

That statement, where our then-president said he was not a literalist, referring to the Bible, well, can you be sure that God sent a son, or *His only begotten Son*. That is how most Americans view Christianity today. They believe that there is a god, but really don't know **the** God of the Bible. That is also the way they believe in Jesus. I know, because that's where I came from. I really thought that the Bible was just a writing from a bunch of guys, not knowing that they were writing under the inspiration of the Holy Spirit.

President Bush went on to say many more things in this interview, more or less saying our belief in Him is why we do good, to be closer to God. But what he said there is not quite true. The Bible says by grace are you saved through faith, not of works less any man boast. The president went on to say that he believed in both evolution and the Bible. If you believe in God and creation you can't believe in evolution. But, again I think most people including Christians also believe this way.

President Bush had an interview with Charles Gibson in 2004 on ABC, when Mr. Gibson (with whom I went to grade school) asked our president the following questions about his faith.

Charles Gibson: "Do we all worship the same God, Christian, Muslim?"

George Bush: "I think we do. We have different routes to getting to the Almighty."

Charles Gibson: "Do Christians, Non-Christians, Muslims, go to heaven in your mind? "

George Bush: "Yes they do, we have *different routes of getting there*. I want you to understand, I want your listeners to understand, I don't get to decide who goes to heaven, the Almighty God decides to who goes to heaven and I am on my personal walk." John 14:6, Jesus said, ***"I am the way the truth, and the life: no man cometh unto the Father, but by me."***

Do you know that the Bible tells us in 2 Peter 1:20–21, ***"Knowing this first, that no prophecy of the scripture is of any private interpretation. For the prophecy came not by the will of man: but holy men of God spake as they were moved by the Holy Ghost."*** The Bible was not written by writings of men, like Joseph Smith wrote *The Book of Mormon*, or the Qu'ran, penned by Muhammad, or Charles T Russell, *The Watch Tower*, or Albert Pike's *Morals and Dogma*. The list of bibles which are not inspired are just books which are not the Word of God. Just because the word *Bible* is written on the covers does not make them holy. And we must be careful as they may not be translated from the original languages, but most important, not speaking the words and guidance from our Majestic Holy Supreme Creator, lover of all mankind, not willing that any should perish, but that all should come to repentance.

Romans 10:17, ***"So than faith cometh by hearing, and hearing by the word of God."***

Ephesians 2:8, ***"For by grace are ye saved through faith; and that not of yourselves: it is the gift of God."***

Hebrews 11:6, ***"But without faith it is impossible to please him: for he that cometh to God must believe that he is, and that he is a rewarder of them that diligently seek him."***

1 Peter 1:23, ***"Being born again, not of corruptible seed, but of incorruptible,*** *by the word of God,* ***which liveth and abideth for ever"*** (emphasis mine). Jesus said in the John3:3 if you're not born again you will not see the kingdom of God.

Re-read both interviews and the answers, and how the president answered those questions. You will find he really didn't believe the Bible and he also believed you didn't have to believe in Jesus. I think he actually believes like most Americans. That is, just leave everyone alone, do what's right in your mind, be what you consider to be a good person, and you'll go to heaven, after all, you earned it.

I think because of all different translations of the Bible many just don't know what to believe. And that because of all the confusion over this brings up a person who just doesn't want to pick up their Bible and read.

CHAPTER FIVE

MAN, THE TEMPLE OF GOD

This chapter should open your eyes insofar as showing you how special you are by letting you see just how much you mean to your Creator. I pray that you will see that you have a more sure word of prophecy, the Holy Bible and how it is relevant in your life. I will condense this teaching, covering what opened my eyes to count things like words, topics and looking for hidden patterns. I believe you will also see in this teaching that the Bible that you probably have somewhere laying around in your home a Book from the Holy Ghost, maybe sitting on your coffee table is not a book written by just a bunch of guys, but it is a book written by holy men of God who were inspired by the Holy Ghost.

In essence, this is a Book from God to you. If you hold to a church tradition that claims to be equal, or overrides the Scriptures, you are not following the Bible. Jesus Christ and the Word are one in the same. John 1:1, 14. Instead of those things that are added onto or go along with the Bible, forget them and get your mind filled of a Book from the Holy Ghost, with a Holy Book directly from the Holy Ghost (Spirit), a part of the Godhead of the Holy Bible.

The world and all creation have a pattern, God's signature. Most of creation contains the Fibonacci spiral. This is the signature of God. Just to review this sequence of numbers where we find the spiral, it starts with 0 and add 1 and you get 1, always adding the last two numbers together. So it's 0, 1, 1, 2, 3, 5, 8, 13, and so on. Let's look at the human ear. There you can see this spiral. Think about this pattern when you read Rom 1:19, ***"Because that which may be known of God is manifest in them; for God hath shewed it unto them. For the invisible things of him from the creation of the world are clearly seen, his eternal power and Godhead so that they are without excuse."*** So right here, anyone can literally see that God put his signature in everything He made.

Looking at what we know to be the largest thing created, the universe, clusters of galaxies to what is known to be the smallest thing created, which is deoxyribonucleic acid, better known as DNA. Through modern technology, even though you cannot see DNA, even with a microscope, we all pretty much know what it looks like. Most of today's detective shows give you a picture of DNA as they are shown in their laboratories looking at DNA evidence that was collected so they can get their man. This DNA is in a Fibonacci spiral. As you see it, it also looks like a winding staircase, or a ladder. This ladder, the rungs of the ladder are measured in what are called angstroms, which is the space between the rungs in the DNA ladder. What you will see is at the base of that DNA, from one rung over to the next rung is 21 angstroms wide and from the bottom of the spiral when it comes back around again. That measurement is 34 angstroms tall, so DNA has the spiral of DNA, has the exact same sequence in it: the Fibonacci sequence.

After King David passed on, his son, King Solomon, built the first temple to worship God. This temple was built under the specifications of God. It was constructed approximately 1000 years before Christ.

Consider this verse today, as it speaks of you. 1 Corinthians 6:19, *"What know ye not that your body is the temple of the Holy Ghost which is in you, which ye have of God, and ye are not your own."*

Here we see that God is telling you that you are now the temple. That in your body, inside of you is the dwelling place of Almighty God. Remember, **God said, let us make man in our own image**, after our likeness. So God spoke man into existence. Man's body is the temple or dwelling place of God, and in this temple resides a copy of the scroll, the Word of God.

Bringing things together, let's look at Psalm 19:1–2, *"The heavens declare the Glory of God; and the firmament sheweth his handiwork. Day unto day uttereth speech, and night unto night sheweth knowledge."*

Remember, the Scriptures were originally written on scrolls that were rolled up like a spiral. The galaxy is a spiral. This picture is showing us and revealing to us the very word of God. Also you will find in Psalm 19, that is goes on to say, *"Their line is gone out through all the earth."* What lines are these? I believe those lines we see in Psalm 19, are the Scriptures.

God is showing that he had Solomon build a temple. Moses erected a tabernacle, which is a portable type of temple, it was the dwelling place of God.

Going back to the temple, I want you to notice that it was built by God's plan. They built it with stones and put it together piece by piece. Think of the human body. The human body is not just one dense solid, it's actually a body that is composed and put together just like the temple was built of stones. We all have these blood cells in our body. We are composed of these tiny little bitty stones called cells. In 1 Peter 2:5 says, "*Ye also, as lively stones, are built up a spiritual house, an holy priesthood, to offer up spiritual sacrifices, acceptable to God by Jesus Christ.*"

Your local church congregation represents the Body of Christ, it's not just one person. One person is not a church. It's a group of people meeting together, worshipping and following the Scriptures. We are the stones that are building the temple of this local congregation. Likewise, all of those who believe in Jesus and trust in the Word of God are the house of God: the lively stones, just like the cells of the body, that make up the temple that you and I dwell in.

Now to get to the count down, the idea of counting things.

We know that we are the temple of God. In the Bible you will find the word temple is found 208 times. Actually, however, it is found a tad more, however it is not describing a temple of worship, but refers to other things, such as a part of the head. So, 208 times the Scriptures mention a place of worship. Did you know that you have 208 bones in your body? Some other sources suggest you have 206, this could be perhaps to the way they count the sternum. The Wikipedia says we have 208 which I believe. It matches the Word of God. If we believe that the skeleton was built by the spoken Word of God, then the skeleton is going to follow a pattern and we should see it in the Scriptures.

Looking at the rib cage, you will find you have a series of ribs on each side. These ribs are joined together in the front by the sternum and in the back by the spine. If you ever counted the bones in your ribcage, you will find you have 12 on each side, and yes, the female has the same number. The ribcage is designed to protect or shield the vital organs of the body. The vital organs are, number 1, the heart. Let's look at the human heart and how many places the Bible refers to it. The heart represents the throne of God. When someone is saved, we say that Jesus dwells in them, or lives inside of their heart. Incidentally, the heart has four chambers. In the Old Testament depiction of the throne of God, which was the ark of the covenant, we see according to the law that God wrote, the ark of the covenant was to be carried by exactly four Levite priests. This is a picture of what Ezekiel chapter 1, and what John saw in Revelation, chapter 4, was four living creatures, of four cherubs that suspended the throne of God. So the heart of mankind literally is the throne of God, where he dwells and where he lives. It's where life emanates from.

In Revelation chapter 4:6, it says, *"**And before the throne there was a sea of glass like unto crystal.**"* Surrounding your heart is a sack of water called the pericardium. That salt water is just the sea surrounding the throne, that's amazing. Next inside the ribcage we have the lungs. We have two lungs that supply the breath we breathe. Breath in the Bible is a picture of the Holy Spirit, the breath of God as we breathe in and out, we're actually supplying oxygen through our heart to the rest of the body. That's what gives us life. If we lose our lungs, if we lose our heart, we will lose our lives.

Speaking of your heart, the throne of God, and also the lungs, the breath of God, you have the 12 white bones on each side of your body, totaling 24 bones and now look at this verse of Scripture. Revelation 4:4 says, *"And round about the throne were four and twenty seats: and upon the seats I saw four and twenty elders sitting, clothed in white raiment."*

So we mentioned the two lungs; they are also a picture of the Old and New Testament of the Bible. They are the seven spirits of God; the Bible says there are seven of these Spirits. Read Isaiah 11:1 and 2. Going back to the two lungs that deliver oxygen to the heart and then through our heart to the blood stream. These blood vessels that go to the heart are in what's called, vascular bundles or nodes. It just so happens that you have seven vascular bundles that take oxygen from the lungs, distribute it from the heart into the blood stream.

Now, let's look at the hand. Take your hand and roll it up, like a fist and aim it at the wall or other object as if you were to hit it. If you look at the top of that fist you will see the Fibonacci Spiral, so our hands are a representation of the signature of God. If you could see an X-ray of your hand with your fingers outstretched, looking at your index finger, you would see that from your knuckle to your finger tip are three bones. You would also find that the first bone from your knuckle to the next bone, to your finger tip have the Fibonacci sequence. In other words, the bone from the knuckle is the same length as the next two bones together. If you could see the bone inside the palm of your hand which connects to the three exposed joints is the same length as the next to bone which it joins. Again, it's the Fibonacci sequence. Your hand was designed by God; it has God's signature in it. This is the same pattern we see throughout God's creation.

Picture that you have opened your Bible and it just so happened it fell open to the first book of the New Testament.

In other words, you would be looking down at the Bible, and on the left side of the Bible you would have the Old Testament and on your right would be the New Testament. I don't know if you know it, but the New Testament has exactly 27 books in it. This New Testament you would be holding with your right hand which so happens, has exactly 27 bones in it. Let's look at a few Scriptures about the right hand.

Exodus 15:6, *"Thy right hand, O Lord, is become glorious in power: thy right hand, hath dashed in pieces the enemy."*

Psalm 17:7, *"Shew thy marvelous lovingkindness, O thou that savest by thy right hand."*

Psalm 60:5, *"Save with thy right hand, and hear me."*.

Psalm 63:8, *"My soul followeth hard after thee: hy right hand upholdeth me."*

Psalm 78:54, *"He hath brought them to the border of his sanctuary, even to this mountain, which his right hand hath purchased."*

See, it's the right hand of God represented by the New Testament and just happens to have 27 books, 27 bones in our hand that represents the saving power. Now think about this: where is Jesus now, according to the Bible? Jesus is sitting at the right hand of God. There's something else in God's right hand.

Isaiah 41:10, says, *"Fear thou not, for I am with thee; be not dismayed; for I am thy God: I will strengthen thee; yea, I will help thee; yea, I will uphold thee with the right hand of my righteousness."*

Let's look at the human spine, speaking of the Fibonacci sequence, has exactly 33 bones in it. That's a picture of Jesus Christ. In Exodus 33, we see Moses. Moses wants to see the face of God. God said no man could see my face and live, so in this 33rd chapter God showed Moses his back parts.

Remember, this is in 33rd chapter, God showed Moses his back, his spine, that just so happens has 33 vertebrae in the spine. Jesus died at the age of 33, so this is a picture of Jesus. Looking at the base numbers of Fibonacci sequence, 1, 1, 2, 3, 5, 8, 13, and add them together you have 33. The very middle of the Bible is Psalm 117. This psalm has two verses, representing the Old and New Testament or the backbone of man. It just so happens that if you add all the words of the 2 verses you come up with 33. The number of vertebrae in the backbone.

Let's look at the human skull, the head. This is where the face is. The skull has 22 bones in it. Let's look at a verse where a skull is mentioned. John 19:17 says, "***And he bearing his cross went forth into a place called the place of a skull, which is called in the Hebrew Golgotha.***" Speaking of the 22 bones, I would like you to see that the number 22 is a number of revelation. In the book of Revelation there are 22 chapters. In Genesis, Abraham offers his only son of promise as a living sacrifice to God, where God supplied a lamb. This gives us a picture of Jesus, our living sacrifice for our sins. Psalm 22:1 says, "***My God, My God, why hast thou forsaken me.***" These are the exact words of Jesus on the cross at the place of the skull. This number 22 shows a picture of revelation as God is now revealed. In the conclusion of Revelation 22, "***There shall be no more curse: but the throne of God and of the lamb shall be in it; and his servants shall serve him: And they shall see his face.***"

Now that we touched on the bones, let's take a closer look at our cells. In every cell of your body you have a similar structure. You have the cell wall, you have all these apparatuses inside the cell and in the middle of the cell you have the cell nucleus. In the cell nucleus, you have 23 pairs of what is called chromosomes, this is where your DNA is stored. In every cell of your body, in the middle of that cell is a nucleus that have 23 pairs, or 46 packages of DNA, called chromosomes. Inside of those chromosomes are bundles of this.

Remember, the DNA spiral is like the Fibonacci spiral has the same pattern, the double helix of the DNA. I think that pretty much of us know what this DNA spiral looks like. We know much of what we learned of DNA in the past fifty years, however, were finding more out each day, so today we're using the findings of what we learned in the past 10 to 15 years. So it's hard to keep up with speed. What we do know today kind of makes one wonder how it is they just can't see that we are created beings, and didn't come about by accident. DNA looks like a spiral ladder, the two rungs of that ladder, or the sides of that ladder are called sugar phosphate back bones. The steps of the ladder, joining the ladder together are called base pairs. They are like a puzzle that join together, they are called base pairs. There are four of these base pairs. There is adenine, thymine, guanine and cytosine. Or to make it simple, A, T, G and C.

Each rung, or step of the DNA has 2 base pairs. These base pairs cannot be mixed. For instance, if you have thymine on one rung, the other half of that ladder has to be adenine. The same holds true for the other two base pair, guanine only goes with cytosine. That's very important, remembering everything in the world has patterns. The joining of these base pairs form what is called genes, hence we get, the genetic code. Isn't it interesting that the first book of the Bible has the word *genes* in it, Genesis, which means "beginnings"? Scientists have discovered the pattern, the sequence of the DNA and therefore we are able to find cancers that they would have never found in years gone by. With their knowledge, they were also able to find that the next sequence is going to form a new gene and the reason why they know that is because between the sequence that makes this gene a part of DNA that they call *stop DNA*.

So, you have a pattern of genes, you have a stop sequence, you have another pattern of genes and a stop sequence. What they found out is that DNA is just like a book that you read. In books, we don't have just one long sentence from the front to the back, but we have periods, stops in between. We put letters down to form words to make sentences, giving directions or thoughts. That's exactly the way DNA is formed. It's written exactly like a book. The genetic scientists are just learning how to read the book. By the way they are, unfortunately learning how to rewrite the book.

Sometime between 2004 and 2006, the University of Ohio released that they had discovered the 22 amino acids. The base pairs joined together to make to form amino acids, these amino acids are the letters in the words and the words joined together to make the gene and the gene sequence is done so there's a period at the end and a new sentence or a new gene sequence is started. The formation of the base pairs forms what is called amino acids. There are exactly 22 of these amino acids that make the letters that make the words that make the sentences which are the genes of the book of your DNA.

What's interesting about this is what we find in the Bible, the book of psalms, chapter 119. This is the longest chapter in the Bible. Because of the length of this chapter it has been divided. It starts with aleph, the first letter of the Hebrew alphabet. As you can see, the next break in the verses is beth, the second letter, and this continues where altogether this happens exactly 22 times for all the letters of the Hebrew alphabet. What is amazing is this is the exact number of amino acids that make the genes that form the book of your DNA.

The discovery that DNA was encoded like a book is only about ten to fifteen years old. I want you to see a Scripture in a book which is about 2,500 years old. In the Old Testament book of Psalms we find Psalm 139:16, *"Thine eyes did see my substance, yet being unperfect; and in thine book all my members were written, which in continuance were fashioned, when as yet there was none of them."*

Consider this. Books don't write themselves, they have an author. Do you think for a moment that the pages of your DNA were just scattered about and through the evolution of time it all came together to put the book of your DNA together? I know this Author and I think you have a pretty good idea yourself. We find this Author in Hebrews 12:2, *"Jesus, the author and finisher of our faith."*

As discussed earlier, the four base pair of your DNA, thymine and adenine, guanine and cytosine can only go together in this pattern, adenine can't match with guanine and the same is true with thymine or adenine matching with cytosine. This has been determined by the Author of the book.

In the book of Isaiah, it's written to seek out the book of the Lord. That's the Word of God and that's the DNA sequence of man. Is. 34:16, *"Seek ye out the book of the Lord, and read: no one of these shall fail, none shall want her mate."*

We can see God is telling Isaiah to write this down, this is going to be a pattern for life; this is the structure of the DNA.

Is that when the base pairs join together, if there's adenine here, there's always thymine here. If cytosine is here, there's always going to be guanine here. If you study the Bible, you know the Old Testament always connects to the New Testament. An example of the two connecting is found in the fourth book of the Bible, the book of Numbers. Here we find that the people are murmuring and sinning against God and God is releasing serpents in and among them that are killing them. They then cry out to God and God tells Moses to make a pole of brass and to put a serpent of brass on it and raise it so the people can look upon it. This will save them from the serpents.

We now go to the New Testament, the 4th book and find in John, chapter 3, "*as Moses lifted up the serpent in the wilderness*", Old Testament, "*even so must the Son of man be lifted up, that whosoever should believe on him should not perish, but have eternal life.*"

You can see by this comparison in the New Testament how it connects perfectly, just as adenine and thymine together with the Old Testament. The interesting thing about the four base pair is thymine is different because when you only have one strand of nucleic acid, it is not deoxyribonucleic acid (DNA); it is ribonucleic acid (RNA). RNA contains adenine, guanine, and cytosine and a fourth base pair called uracil. When you add the second strand of the RNA, it becomes DNA and uracil is removed and replaced with the chemical thymine. So this gives us a picture of the four Gospels. They all give us a picture of Jesus, but one is different. Just like the four base pair, but one is different. Matthew, Mark, and

Luke have a similar story and are called the Synoptic Gospels because they seem to synchronize. John's Gospel is different. Like the base pair above, three synchronize, but thymine is different.

Now, going back to DNA, we see it looks like spiral stair case. This is the Fibonacci spiral which looks like a ladder. Thinking of a story in the Bible with a ladder we would come across

Genesis 28:12, *"And he dreamed, and behold a ladder setup on the earth, and the top of it reached to heaven: and behold, the angels of God ascending and descending upon it."*

Now I want you to notice the description of the ladder given to us. This ladder is none other—remember DNA and the Word of God and everything—this ladder is none other than Jesus Christ. Let's look at John 1:51, *"Hereafter ye shall see heaven open, and the angels of God ascending and descending upon the Son of man."* Jesus Christ is literally the ladder; hence, He is the Word of God, and hence He is the book of life in our DNA. Notice 2 Corinthians 3 says, *"Forasmuch as you are manifestly declared to be the epistle of Christ ministered by us, written not in with ink, but with the Spirit of the living God; not in tables of stone, but in fleshly tables of the heart."* The law was written on stone tablets by God. So today we have His words written on our hearts. That's the reason we feel convicted when we do or say something wrong: God wrote it in our hearts. And that is also true when people do wrong things: their heart is hardened, just like the stone tablets Moses received from God.

Remember what our cells are. Our cells are the stone building blocks that make up the temple of God. Romans

2:15 says, *"Which show the work of the law,* [the 10 commandments] *written in their hearts, their conscience also bearing witness, and their thoughts the mean while, accusing or else excusing one another."* God says that the law was literally written in our hearts.

Luke 4:4 says, *"And Jesus answered him, it is written, That man shall not live by bread alone, but by every word of God."* Luke 8: 11, says, *"The seed is the Word of God."* Here we should think of a seed that you physically plant into the ground. The seed you plant has the DNA of whatever type of seed you plant. If you plant a seed for an apple tree, you shouldn't look for oranges on that tree.

Seed is also a biblical term that refers to literally the seed of mankind which contains His DNA. And so in this parable in Luke chapter 8, Jesus himself is saying, that seed is the Bible. He's saying that our DNA is the Bible.

This takes us back to the temple of Solomon. We see this in 1 Kings 7. Solomon erected two pillars in the front of this temple. Think of that number two, we have the two sides of DNA, we have the two testaments of the Bible, we have the two lungs, and the seven spirits of God.

First Kings 7:21, *"And he set up the pillars in the temple: and called the name thereof Jachin: and he set up the left pillar, and called the name thereof Boaz."* According to the measurements given to us in the Scriptures, both pillars are each exactly 23 cubits tall. Our DNA, the chromosomes, contain 23 pairs or 46 altogether. In Genesis 2: 23 you see that God created man and God made woman from the man. God then brought her unto the man, notice what Adam said, Genesis 2:23, *"And Adam said, this is now bone of my bones, and flesh of my flesh: she shall be called Woman because she was taken out of Man. Therefore shall a man leave his father and his mother, and shall cleave unto his wife: and they shall be one flesh."*

What Adam is saying here is when a man and woman come together, nine months later they become one flesh because the miracle of conception is that 23 chromosomes are taken from the man and 23 from the woman and they're joined together to make a baby inside the womb of the mother.

I hope to accomplish two things in this chapter. One, to show how God's creation is all around us, by seeing His signature right in front of our eyes, and showing us that we are His living temple. I also want to emphasize the importance of counting things. Through counting things, you can actually see God's hand in most everything.

In 1 Corinthians 3:16–17 says, *"Know ye not that ye are the temple of God, and that the Spirit of God dwelleth in you? If any man defile the temple of God, him shall God destroy; for the temple of God is holy, which temple ye are."*

Adam spoke exactly 46 words about Eve, describing the conception and nature of life inside of a woman's womb. The forty-sixth book of the Bible is where we find that we are the temple of God. Jesus told the people around Him, *"Destroy this temple and in thee days I will rebuild it."* They didn't know that He was referring to the temple of his body.

And John 2:20 says, *"Then said the Jews, Forty and six years was this temple in building, and wilt thou rear it up in three days? But he spake of the temple of his body."*

Is it just by accident that there are 46 chromosomes that contain our DNA in every cell of our body? The forty-sixth book of the Bible, which is 1 Corinthians, is where we are told that we are the temple of God. This number 46 is consistently linked with the temple and the tabernacle that we see in the Scriptures.

So think of this. We have the 2 rungs of DNA, the sides of DNA; they're joined together by the 4 base pairs and they're contained in the 46 chromosomes. The Old Testament was written in Hebrew, which has 22 letters. The New Testament was written in Greek, which has 24 letters, which wouldn't you know it, totals 46. Could it be by design? I think so.

Going back to the Old Testament, in the book of Exodus, in chapter 25, God gives Moses the instructions on how to build the tabernacle, exactly the way it is depicted in heaven in Revelation 4, with the 24 elders and the throne of God and the 7 spirits of God. So what's in heaven He'll match on Earth. That, by the way, is what Jesus prayed, *"Thy will be done on earth as it is in heaven."* So God wanted Moses to build an earthly tabernacle, a temple, literally, so God could dwell inside or with His people. In the tabernacle were four pillars, like the four base pairs, adenine, guanine, cytosine and thymine. Down the south side and the north side, each had 20 boards, and there were 6 boards across the back. That is 46 boards in total with the entrance way consisting of 4 pillars which match the 4 base pairs. I believe that we literally are the tabernacle of Almighty God.

I want to look at the 23rd book of the Bible for a moment, which is the book of Isaiah. In chapter 53 it enumerates everything that Christ did for us as a sacrifice on the cross, with words like, *"Surely he hath born our griefs, and carried our sorrows: yet we did esteem him stricken, smitten of God, and afflicted. But he was wounded for our iniquities: the chastisement of our piece was upon him; and with his stripes we are healed."*

If you notice, starting with what was accomplished on the cross, starting with the word born, you have exactly 46 things (words explaining) that which were done. This is found in the 23rd book. Remember, there are 23 base pairs of these 46 chromosomes are the packages where our DNA is stored. The DNA looks like the Fibonacci sequence, the spiral. Do you remember the caduceus? The caduceus was an early ancient emblem. The 46 chromosomes, called X chromosomes, which kind of resemble a cross. This cross (X chromosomes) have our spiral DNA around it. Remember the fourth book in the Old Testament, the book of Numbers and what it matched the New Testament? They're joined together. Looking at John 3 to refresh your memory, *"As Moses lifted up the serpent in the wilderness, even so must the Son of Man be lifted up."* That is an exact replica of the DNA strands inside of the 46 cross that are in your cell.

In Genesis 3, Satan spoke 46 words to Eve, the mother of all humanity. Those 46 words, I believe, represent the 46 chromosomes, which I believe represent the sin that is in all of mankind. Think back on the 46 things Christ nailed on the cross.

I want to thank Pastor Michael Hoggard for his studies on this comparison of the Bible and the makeup of man. And also for this chapter that not only opened my heart to the KJV Bible but opened my mind to the importance of counting things. This teaching is much deeper than what I shared with you. If you would like to receive this teaching in greater detail I suggest you write to him at the address I shared in the previous chapter, where I opened with a small segment of this teaching.

CHAPTER SIX

NUMEROLOGY

As a Christian, this is one chapter that I really did not want to research or write about, therefore I will not go into great detail on numerology as I believe it is demonic at the core. In many circles it is considered to be a science, as that title is after all dealing with numbers. Also, this is really the same thing as astrology and fortune telling. The dictionary defines them both as determining one's future, and how to predict your course of life.

This coming from the "American College Dictionary"

Numerology – The study of numbers (as one's birth year) supposedly to determine their influence on ones' life and future.

Astrology – A study or science which assumes, and professes to interpret, the influence of the heavenly bodies on human affairs. 2) (Formerly) practical astronomy, the earliest form of the science.

I could finish this chapter right here. The reason I make this statement is because I am familiar what the Scriptures have to say about this topic. I would rather trust what God wants for my life than look at how the stars are aligned or count up the numbers associated with my name and the numbers referring to my birth date, day and year. God said in Jer. 29:11, *"**For I know the thoughts that I think toward you, saith the LORD, thoughts of peace, and not of evil, to give you an expected end.**"*

Numerology and astrology go hand in hand, both entwined in the occult. They both, after all, rely on each other, and both are an abomination to the Lord. In doing a ground-floor study on this topic, I asked my local librarian for a book on the study of numbers. The librarian said, "Oh you want numerology." I quickly responded "no," knowing somewhat what numerology was about. But then I realized that this was exactly what I needed. After all, the basic scheme of what we are reading about all deals with numbers. This world is not a Christian world, even though Jesus loved it and died for it. This world never really received Him, therefore they really don't know Him.

The next thing I did was to check out five books dealing with this topic. The books I took out were *The Complete Book of Numerology* by Joyce and Jack Keller; *The Numbers Book* by Sepharial; *The Little Giant Encyclopedia of Numerology* by Daniel Heydon; and one title that I found interesting, *Your Days Are Numbered* by Florence Campbell. What jumped out at me was that my subtitle for this book is *Our Days Are Numbered*. The last of the five books is *The Secret Science of Numerology* by Shirley Blackwell Lawrence. These books are important for this study because in the first and second chapters of this book I laid out the idea of numbers dealing with currency, structures and such. If one looks into these things, they will find that the numbers used have their foundation tied into numerology and the occult.

I thought I would be able to quickly skim through the five books and have the answers to what I wanted. I found on further review of these books that there were a lot of similarities, and yet some seemed to arrive at different opinions with different methods to get there. What I am saying is that these books needed to be read through in their entirety and studied to really know what the authors wanted you to digest. Before I continue, I want you to know that I did not do this study to that extreme. One thing more I would like to say about the authors is they seemed to be spiritual, insofar as with their prayers, thanking God and so on. The only thing wrong was that they were getting their help from another source, another god.

At this point I would like to give you a couple of scriptures to support what I'm saying regarding guiding your life with astrology and/or numerology. Jeremiah, 10:23 says, *"O LORD, I know that the way of man is not in himself: it is not in man that walketh to direct his steps."* Another that many are familiar with is Proverbs 3:6, *"In all thy ways acknowledge him, and he shall direct thy paths."*

Astrology and numerology are nothing more than witchcraft or workers dealing with familiar spirits looking to find what their future holds, without looking to who holds the future. Looking to the stars or numbers to find direction for ones' life is evil at the core, so if you are involved quit, and repent, turn away from that and let God direct your life.

In my study, I just so happened to look up one of the authors, of the books I took out of the library, *The Numbers Book*, the author, Sepharial. This book was not his only book. His name was actually Dr. Walter Gorn Old. He was in the inner sanctum of Theosophical Society. Sepharial wrote many books, and by the title of his books you will understand where his heart was. After all, it's written, Matthew 12:34, "*For out of the abundance of the heart the mouth speaketh.*" I will list a few of his many books so I can show you what I alluded to, *The New Dictionary of Astrology; The Kaballah of Numbers; A Manual of Occultism; Cosmic Symbolism.* and *Science of Foreknowledge.*

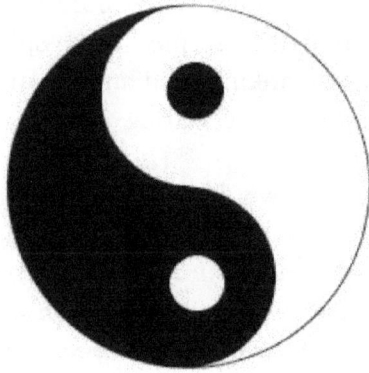

One of the other books I checked out, was *The Secret Science of Numerology* by Shirley Blackwell Lawrence. The title of chapter six jumped out at me. The chapter, "As Above So Below," had another meaning to me, this dealing with opposites. The topic of the book itself is numerology, which is nothing more than dealing with the occult. This in turn brought to mind a couple of things. The first of yin yang teaching on opposites, such as night and day, good and bad right and wrong and so on. Many cults stem from yin yang as it is in itself a religion, dealing with Chinese philosophy.

Another form of this is found in the pagan symbol of Baphomet where this idol is filled with opposites and even points with different hands to above and below.

The figure above is half man and half woman, half animal and half man. As you study this picture carefully you can see that it doesn't stop there. This very image sits in the church of Satan. Though you cannot see from this image, tattooed on each arm are Latin words, on the left is *SOLVE* (separate) and on the right is *COAGULA* (join together). It is the image of the head which is found in the upside-down pentagram.

This pentagram has a great deal of significance with satanic worship, as well as many other symbols that we the public are unaware of. These type of activities are given birth from such things as astrology and numerology.

Continuing with numerology, I found that there are what are called master numbers. These are double digit numbers, such as 11, 22, 33, and so on. These type numbers represent the positive and the negative, male, female, again opposites, as all the above symbols represent. Such numbers have a certain power as for instance the number is a follower; however, the 11 likes to stand on its own two feet. In numerology, according to author Lawrence all 11's are meant to be professional people, for they cannot be happy in mundane work. Their desire is to uplift others through the beauty of their creations or with their inspired thoughts.

These are what are known as the, as Above numbers because of their intuitive and inspirational thoughts. These type of what seem to be life patterns and structural patterns, however, have nothing to do with direction from God and have much to do with chance hanging on numbers or a star.

One more thing which is addressed in all the books I listed above is the numbered chart used to get the numbers that in actuality predict your future and your path in life. Below is that chart.

NUMEROLOGY

1	2	3	4	5	6	7	8	9
A	B	C	D	E	F	G	H	I
J	K	L	M	N	O	P	Q	R
S	T	U	V	W	X	Y	Y	

Numerical value of each

Each row is a list of letters. the numbers above are the numbers you are to use to find the number value of that letter. For example, the letters *E*, *N*. and *W*, all are the number 5. The above chart is used to break, say, your name down to numbers. Working that with your birth day, date and year, you will learn through their forecast just how to find what job you are meant to have, who you are to be married to, and so on.

Or you could just pray to God for direction. Oh how simple that would be. After all, He does direct your path. One more thing, if you notice the number 6 above and look at the letters in that roll spell fox which adds up to 666, do you think that might have happened on purpose? If you remember back in the first chapter of this book we mentioned that Rupert Murdoch was a member of the Bohemian Club. This group gets together and make big plans for the New World Order.

There are so many scriptures that tell us there is a way that seems right to man, but that is the way to death. Read Proverbs 14:12. We need to walk by faith, faith in His word. I cannot put all the scriptures down about how we are to get our guidance from God without going to a thirty-page chapter. I will add one more thought on this topic of numerology, as to how God sees it.

First Kings 23:24 says, *"Moreover the workers withfamiliar spirits, and the wizards, and images, and the idols, and all the abominations that were spied in the land of Judah and in Jerusalem, did Josiah put away, that he might perform the words of the law which were written in the book that Hilkiah the priest found in the house of the LORD."*

Before I close out this chapter, I would like to discuss what is sometimes called Bible numerology. The difference with this numerology is you don't need to figure out any numbers, there already there in your Bible. In the Bible there are literal numbers that refer to certain things. Seeing what those numbers are referring to, you can see what they symbolize. That is how the numerical chart in chapter two was created. An example of this is Jesus fasted forty days and was tempted. In Genesis we find that it rained for forty days and forty nights. Moses went up into the mount for forty days and nights when he received the commandments of God. The children of Israel wandered in the desert for forty years.

In these examples we learn that the number forty has to do with trials and temptations. Look again at chapter two.

1 Peter 4:7 3 . . . "But the end of all things is at hand: be ye therefore sober, and watch unto prayer."

CHAPTER SEVEN

EVENTS AND DATES POSSIBLY REVEALING END TIMES

Over the last few chapters I showed two dates that seem to point to end time events: March 13, 2013 and September 11, 2001. March 13 was discussed in chapter 3 when on the 13th day of the 3rd month and the 13th year, the smoke came through the chimney in which Pope Francis was elected pope. This brought the possible false prophet on the scene. In the last chapter we found that in the first book of the Bible, the 11th chapter, verse 9 was the last we've heard of the Tower of Babel. This tower came to an end. This was found in the 1st book of the Bible which I found to be interesting, as it could indicate the year, as the towers came to an end on 9/11/01. I found it very interesting that the Babel tower is last heard of in verse 9 in the 11th chapter in the 1st book of the Bible. On this September date the United States was changed as our towers came down and so did our US Constitution.

9/11 not only effected our liberties and our rights, but it changed our way of thinking around the world. We are actually willing to give up our privacy to get *government security*. I have actually heard a few of our political figures say, "never let a crisis go to waste." One even went so far as to put the word *good* in when he said, "never let a good crisis go to waste." If I'm not mistaken, it was said by Chicago Mayor, Rahm Emmanuel. I apologize to Mayor Emmanuel if I misquoted him, but I'm quite sure it was him. The other politician was Hillary Clinton. These were made on the platform of safety and security for the protection of the American people. We the people have been looking away from what the government is doing, while our Constitution is being stripped away. Starting with the Patriot Act, and bringing in the NDAA and Agenda 21. Our country is being changed, and what's scary is the masses don't seem to care as long as they stay in their own world. The only problem is that their world will be changed and then there will be nothing you can do about it as you will no longer have a voice to make a difference.

Finding those above dates which seem to link events together with Scripture really made me start to wonder if I could possibly find other verses that might give some credence to the two I found. Keep in mind that these Scriptures don't necessarily mean that this is some kind of Bible Code. I just see it as interesting and hope you do as well. After all, God does speak to us through His Word. If you are anything like me, you can see all that is happening around us and know we are living in the end times according to Scriptures already written without the mention of what I'm writing about .

I never had expected to write on this topic, until I found those two events where the Scripture verses matched the dates and it sparked my curiosity. I thought these dates to be world changing events, and they made me wonder if I could find other world events that paralleled Scripture. I did find some verses that seemed to match dates that made me think that I'm stretching things out of context to make the Scriptures fit the events of what happened in these world news events. I did not want to be reaching for something that wasn't there, but what I found did make me think maybe it was showing something that is there and can only be found after it is revealed. In other words, world news that is shaping our end-time scenario.

Let me explain. As previous mentioned, I read the book from Tom Horn and Cris Putnam, which I mentioned in the second chapter entitled "The Final pope is here, Petrus Romanus." This book is not Bible prophecy, but I thought it to be interesting. Years earlier, a book entitled *Prophecy of the Popes* was written in the eleventh century, by Archbishop Malachy. The book may have been altered over the years, but it still kept in line with what was happening with the sequence of the popes. In this book, Bishop Malachy supposedly named and numbered all the popes from his time to the end time false prophet, which will be the 112th. The 112th pope now sits in office. In the Old Testament book of Hosea, I found in the 13th chapter and the 3rd verse, where it says, *"as smoke out of the chimney."* This verse seems to match the ceremony at the Vatican in which they emit either black smoke through the chimney if they have not found a pope or white smoke if a pope was found.

On the13th of March they never did emit black smoke as the first time the smoke came through the chimney it was white and Pope Francis surfaced. Going back, those numbers or dates if reversed could be written 3-13 or March 13th which would coincide with the 9/11/01. Keep in mind that Hebrew is read from right to left while here in the US and most other countries we read from left to right which could explain why the verse is before the chapter.

I did pray about finding other world-changing events where the date would or could coincide with the Scripture. I believe that the last two dates to be world-changing events. I started to think of all the things going on in our world today that would be considered world changing. The thought that came to mind was Fukushima. The reason I thought of this event is that I have followed world news events and believe that this disaster is responsible for the radiation being detected in the snow that fell in the US during this long winter. Doing some research on this disaster I found that it was Friday, March 11, 2011 a magnitude 9.0 earthquake occurred off the coast of Tokohu, Japan, creating a tsunami. This quake is referred to as The Great East Japan Earthquake, and also known as the 2011 Tohoku earthquake. It was the most powerful earthquake ever to hit Japan since we've been recording earthquakes. It's the fifth largest in recorded history. This quake moved Honshu, the main island of Japan, 8 feet east and shifted the earth's axis by estimates of 4 to 10 inches and generated sound waves detected by the low orbiting **GOCE** satellite. This acronym stands for the Gravity Field and Steady-State Ocean Circulation Explorer.

The tsunami created by this quake sent 133-foot waves crashing into the Fukushima Daiichi Nuclear Power Plant complex. This caused a level-7 meltdown to three reactors. Since this disaster, radiation from this is still in the area reaching the United States. Also, not to mention, over 300 gallons of contaminated water has been spilling from these reactors every day since the meltdown right up to this date. My information says that this water is reaching just off the shores of California. All this information seems to me as an end time disaster, so I looked in the Scriptures to see if I could find something pointing to this event.

In the New Testament Book of James, chapter 3, verse 11 says, *"Doth a fountain send forth at the same place sweet water and bitter?"* Looking at this verse I could see 3 as the month of March and the 11 as the date and also the year, but it was the opposite of what I found in the Old Testament when I found 11/9 and the 13/3. At this time, I did not make the connection of the Hebrew and the Greek. Then I remembered that the New Testament was written in Greek, and like us they read and write from left to right, so this did fit. I found a couple of other scriptures that might have to do with these bitter waters. The first is in the Old Testament book of Proverbs chapter 5, verse 4, which says, *"but her end as* bitter_*as wormwood, sharp as a two-edged sword."* This verse is speaking of destruction. In Revelation 11:8 says; *"And the name of the star is called Wormwood: and the third part of the waters became wormwood; and many men died of the waters, because they were made bitter."*

What I also found to be interesting in the book of Proverbs was that chapter 5 and verse 4 can be added together which is 9, which was the size of the earthquake which caused this disaster. However, in all of this I could be just reaching for things. I think it is something to consider.

I still have doubts, insofar as am I just trying to make things fit to what I think could be something, or is there really something there? While lying in bed I tried to think of some date I knew that was earth-shattering and still effects our lives today and reaches into not just our present but also our future. While lying there, I did recall such an event that this day is etched into my brain. The date, December 7, 1941 is remembered as a date in infamy. I started looking for this by searching the Bible for the word war or wars. There was only one verse I found that could fit this particular date and that was found in the book of Revelation, 12:7 which could fit December 7. Was I reaching for something that wasn't there and trying to make it fit? This verse says, *"And there was war in heaven: Michael and his angels fought against the dragon; and the dragon fought against his angels."* I thought that maybe this fits; after all, this is a start to a war.

Thinking of what I thought would describe current events, I noticed that the three events I had found also indicated not just the month and day but also included the year. I decided to do some research on the attack on Pearl Harbor to see if I could find some other reasons for the attack than just sinking ships and taking lives. What I found was Japan wanted control of the Pacific. While the US naval forces were stationed in Hawaii, this posed a threat against their fight to conquer China. They knew if they could wipe out the naval forces in Hawaii they would have about 18 months before the US could retaliate at Pearl Harbor. What they did not know was that the navy sent their aircraft carriers out at that time on routine patrol.

Another reason for the attack was twofold, Pearl Harbor was about half the distance as the United States. And second, they thought they could get back to their mainland before the United States knew what hit them. Another reason was that there was an oil embargo by the US, and whatever they were going to do to control the Pacific would have to be done quickly.

There is much more to this attack and the start to this war, but I did find it interesting that Japan wanted to control the Pacific and the US was in their way. With this in mind, I did find a verse which I believe fits this scenario. Because of the date, and thinking of the how the first book of the Bible could apply to the year, I decided to just look at the forty-first book of the Bible, which was the year of the attack. Again, you may not agree with me, nor could I say, "Here it is."

Looking at the twelfth chapter, which would indicate the month, Jesus is giving a parable of the wicked husbandmen (farmer). This parable is talking of a certain man who planted a vineyard and set a hedge around it, and dug a place for the wine vat, and built a tower. He rented it out to a farmer to care for it and then went to a far land. When harvest time came and rent was due, he sent a servant to collect the rent. As the parable continues, they kept beating and at times killing the servants who were sent to collect the rent. As they came to collect the rent they would throw rocks at them This could be modern-day missiles or bombs, and even at times killing them rather than paying the rent. In verse 7 of this chapter it says, ***"But those husbandmen said among themselves, this is the heir; come, let us kill him, and the inheritance shall be* ours."**

Mark is the 41st book in the Bible, chapter 12 and verse 7. That's 12/7/41. This could fit the day of infamy: The Japanese attack on Pearl Harbor. Maybe I'm reaching again, but I see what I'm seeing because of where I found it. I see the husbandmen the (farmers) as the Japanese army. The son who is heir are our naval forces, after all Hawaii became a state on August 21, 1959; thereby our US Navy was heir to the land. Japan wanted control of the Pacific and with our ships there it would be impossible. Therefore, they sent the husbandmen to kill the heir. Again I could be just trying to make things fit, but even without this we know our time is short.

At this time, I would like to show how verses and chapter do seem to point to happenings in the Bible. The Bible is a collection of 66 books, 39 in the Old Testament and 27 in the New. What is most interesting about this is in the Old Testament book of Isaiah, we have exactly 66 chapters that match the 66 books of the Bible. The first chapter of Isaiah, verse two says, *"Hear, O heavens, and give ear, O earth: for the Lord hath spoken. I have nourished and brought up children, and they have rebelled against me."* This coincides with the opening of Genesis with Adam and Eve. The fortieth book of the Bible is Matthew, the first book opening the New Testament. The fortieth chapter of Isaiah opens with this, *"Comfort ye, comfort ye my people, saith your God. "Speak ye comfortably to Jerusalem, and cry unto her, that her warfare is accomplished, that her iniquity is pardoned."* As the first chapter matched the first book so the 40th chapter matched the opening of the 40th book. So it is with the last couple of chapters of Isaiah where we find judgment just as in the 66th book of the Bible, **Revelation,** when judgment begins. The entire book of the prophet Isaiah was the most complete findings of the famous discovery of the Dead Sea scrolls found in 1947. I believe that this finding was a major event in history. If I had the exact date I would look for a matching date in the Scriptures.

With the verses and chapters being important as shown above, I did come across a few more dates in recent history that appear to relate to scriptures in the Bible. One that I will share with you is found 1 Kings 2:5–6, *"Moreover thou knowest also what Joab the son of Zeruiah did to me, and what he did to the two captains of the host of Israel, unto Abner the son of Ner, and unto Amasa the son Jether, whom he slew, and shed the blood of war in peace, and put blood of war upon his girdle that was about his loins, and in his shoes that were on his feet. Do therefore according to the wisdom, and let not his hoar head go down to the grave in peace."*

The above, I believe, could be speaking also of Osama bin Laden. It was on the *May 2, 2011*that Osama bin Laden was captured and executed. The above scripture alludes to a man filled with the blood of others, that his gray head go down to the grave in horror. As shown above in the *2nd chapter, the 5th verse, the 11th* book of the bible is where we see this man who admitted to the killings of 9/11 being put to death. This man had the blood of many on his person and is the founder of the radical group, al-Qaeda. I believe this group to be Satanic.

I will show you why I believe Satan was behind this attack and wanted to show his hand on 9/11. To start with, the twin towers looked like a giant 11. Both buildings were **110** stories tall. The very first plane to strike on 9/11 was flight 11. This flight struck just above the 92nd floor, 9 + 2 = 11. From the 92nd floor up, the escape route was destroyed. There were 11 in the fight crew. There were also 5 terrorists aboard with the flight crew and the 76 passengers, the total number of people was 92, 9 + 2 = 11. The number 9/11 added together 9 + 1 + 1 = 11. The first tower struck was the first to fall, it fell at 10:28 a.m. Add the 10 to the 28 is 38, 3 + 8 = 11. Let's continue looking at the flights involved in this attack. There was Flight 11. The second plane that struck the south tower was Flight 175, with 65 aboard, and that's 6 + 5 = 11.

The third plane was Flight 77 that struck the pentagon and Flight 93 that crashed just outside Shanksville, PA. After I tell you something about these flights, you probably will never forget the flight numbers again. Think of flight 11, then will go to flight 93, 9 + 3 = 12. Now we will go to flight 175, 1 + 7 + 5 = 13. And of course flight 77, 7 + 7 = 14, that's 11, 12, 13 and 14. I don't think these terrorist gave any thought as to what flight numbers they were hijacking and just what flight number would crash into which designated target.

Couldn't Flight 11 have been the second plane to crash or could not it have targeted the Pentagon? Flight 77 hit the Pentagon, which is a 77-foot-tall structure just off highway 77. Do you think these terrorist took that into consideration? Not for a second. Also Flight 77 had 6 in the flight crew and had 5 terrorists, added together we get another 11. Flight 93 consisted of a crew of 7 and 4 terrorists. once again added we come up with 11. One thing more about this flight is there were, in addition, 33 passengers, which is a number related to different occults Altogether, the combined number of people on all four flights came to 227. Add those numbers together that's 2 + 2 + 7 = 11. Also on that day, not only the Twin Towers came down, but building number 7, which was a 47-story building. That's 4 + 7 = 11. This building happened to have 47,000 square feet of office space on each floor. Adding the 4 and 7, we come up with another 11. I think Satan showed his hand. If you counted the total number 11s up to this point, it's 13, another satanic number. It's all over our dollar bill, I think 19, times, which was the total number of terrorist on the 4 flights.

Ephesians 6:12 says, ***"For we wrestle not against flesh and blood, but against principalities, against powers,*** *against the rulers of the darkness of this world, against spiritual wickedness in high places. "*

It was estimated there were some 2,900 office workers lost in twin towers. That's 2 + 9 = 11. However, I won't count this 11, as there were many more lives lost. This also does not take into account the undetermined number of pedestrians on the street below, the 343 firefighters, the 72 police officers, and the 227 total people in the four flights. Therefore, this was a satanic attack as we see the repetitive use of 11. Satan is stepping up his warfare as he knows he's on short time.

Revelation 12:12, *"Woe to the inhabiters of the earth and of the sea! For the devil is come down unto you, having great wrath, because he knoweth that he hath but a short time. "*

Luke 21:36, *"Watch ye therefore, and pray always, that ye may be accounted worthy to escape all these things that shall come to pass, and to stand before the Son of man. "*

On April 19, 2011, the famous dictator of Cuba, Fidel Castro, resigned as the communist leader after 45 years. Earlier in life Castro was popular with the people of Cuba as he rebelled against the communist leadership of the dictator, Batista. He eventually overthrew Batista in January 1959, shortly after he became leader at the age of 32. One of the last things he did, after meeting with Pope Benedict, was to seem to give more religious freedom to the people of Cuba. Wondering what his thoughts might be and what the Scriptures said, if anything, relative to this man and him stepping down, I went to the 11th book of the Bible, the 4th verse and the 19th chapter, 1 Kings 19:4, *"It is enough; now O Lord take away my life; for I am not better than my fathers."* Matching this verse with this man is an assumption, but nevertheless, I did find it interesting.

Of all significant dates in our recent history, the one date that I think to be the most important to the whole world is, May 14, 1948, the day that Israel became a nation. Looking at the 48th book of the Bible which is the book of Galatians, the 5th chapter, verse 14, that's 5/14/48. Remember in the Old Testament the number of the day is first and in the New Testament the month is first determining the books and the chapters and the last is always the sequential location number or the place where that book is located in the Bible representing the year. One other thing I would like to mention before we look at that verse is the two places where I did not mention a book number. In the Book of Hosea 13:3 (Old Testament), speaking of the smoke through the chimney. And in James 3:11 (New Testament), James speaks of the bitter water. In both incidents, the 13 and the 11 are both mentioning the day, and I found that they could also be implied to mean the year. Going back to the 5th chapter, the 14th verse in the 48th book, it says, *"For all the law is fulfilled in one word, even to this; thou shalt love thy neighbor as thyself."*

At first glance I really didn't see this as matching the date until I read it over a couple of times. The law was originally given to the Jews, hence the law. But the law also alludes to the Word of God. The entire Bible is actually the law. I see Israel becoming a state as a fulfillment of the word or the law. Ever since Israel became a state, it became hated more than its people, if that could have possibly happened, which it did. Therefore, I can really see this verse applying to the date Israel became a nation. I also see the verse just before that verse to substantiate my findings. 5:13 opens with this, *"For brethren,"* [Israel], *"ye have been called unto liberty."* Liberty means freedom. They finally have their own land after over 2,500 years, a place where they are their own, and a place of liberty.

DATES POSSIBLY REVEALING END TIMES TETRAD, FOUR BLOOD MOONS

I would like to give you a brief look into the much talked-about in Christian circles, the tetrad. In the Gospel of Luke 21:25 says. *"And there shall be signs in the sun, and the moon, and in the stars; and upon the earth distress of nations, with perplexity; the seas and the waves roaring."* There are other verses discussing this phenomenon found in Joel, 2:31, Acts, 2:20 and Revelation 6:12. In all these verses it mentions that there will also be signs in the stars, whereas these particular blood moons have nothing to do with the stars. A tetrad is a series of lunar or solar eclipses. What seems so special about this tetrad is that all the lunar eclipses occur on consecutive Jewish holy days. I know of three books on this topic that are available at your local Christian book store or on the internet at Amazon. com. I have not read on this topic; therefore, I do not have much to say. I did see an interview with Mark Blitz who was on the Christian television program *Prophecy in the News*, with host Gary Stearman. I did find it to be interesting.

The discussion brought up Genesis chapter 1 verse 14 where it says the sun and the moon were given to us as *signs,* seasons, days and years. How many times I read that verse, yet I never paid attention to the fact that the first thing mentioned was the signs. Most everyone knows of their importance to God, that He knows every hair on your head, you are also engraved upon His hands, which is found in Is. 49:16.

Even so is the importance of all his creation that he also knows every star and He calls them by their names, Psalm 147:4. It's also written in Psalm 19:1, *"The heavens declare the glory of God; and the firmament sheweth his handywork."*

On April 8, 2014 an event occurred that happens roughly every 2 years, 48 days. That is when the Earth, Mars and the sun align and Mars is quite visible with the naked eye. What's so remarkable about this event is that it was precisely one week before the first of the four blood moons that most all the planet saw, either outside or on worldwide news. This occurred on April, 15, which was the Jewish feast of Passover. There are many Christians who believe these blood moons will usher in the end of days and the second coming of our Savior, Jesus Christ. Others believe that this tetrad will not necessarily usher in the return Jesus, but will bring some other event, perhaps war with Israel, as the last two tetrads are related to wars occurring in Israel.

Let me explain. In 1948, the Jews conquered the land which is now known as Israel. During the Jewish calendar year that starts in the spring of one year and ends in the fall of the next, overlapping our Gregorian calendar that starts and ends in the middle of winter. This tetrad year on our calendar was 1949 and this was the first since 1493 when the Jews were expelled from France and during the timeline of the famous voyage of Christopher Columbus. The Tetrad after the one occurring in 1949 was in 1967, during the Six-Day War in Israel when the Jews conquered Jerusalem.

It's my understanding that the next tetrad is approximately five hundred years from the conclusion of our tetrad in 2015. According to NASA, this is a highly unusual tetrad; a succession of total blood-red lunar eclipses each followed by six full moons which all conclude on September 28, 2015. Keep in mind that this alignment only happened a handful of times in the last two thousand years.

It's important to keep in mind that the first mention of these tetrads was by NASA and wasn't conjured by religious zealots. It was in 2008 that Mark Blitz started talking about the tetrad, so I do believe he was the first of the Christian authors who picked up on this event and related it to the Scriptures. If this tetrad ushers in and/or show us a great event, I don't think we will have to wait too long.

What seems to be so important about this is the rarity of these blood moons occurring on Jewish holy days. It seems that it has only happened two times in the last five hundred years, at which time the nation of Israel has been at war. The tetrads were in 1949/1950 and 1967/1968. As stated earlier, Israel became a nation in May, 1948 and warred against its neighbor for approximately the next two years to hold onto their land. In 1967 was the Six-Day War for the capture of Jerusalem. Both of these blood moons came in the mist of Israel in the beginning of war or during an Israeli war. Could this possibly be a sign of a coming war?

Luke 21:20-21, *"And when ye shall see Jerusalem compassed with armies, then know that the desolation thereof is nigh. Then let them which are in the mountains; and let them which are in the midst of it depart out; and let not them that are in the countries enter there into."*

Let's buckle our seat belt as we watch and pray.

Jer. 33:3 . . . "Call unto me, and I will answer thee, and I shew thee great and mighty things, that thou knowest not."

CHAPTER EIGHT

INTRODUCTION TO CHAPTER 9 PATTERNS

Patterns are found throughout the Scriptures if you look for them. We found in the second chapter of this book that patterns helped us to determine what a specific number would relate to. A pattern was laid out in the very opening of our Bible with the seven days of creation. It is with the pattern of our seven-day week that we can not only measure our weeks, but our months and years. It's with this simple pattern we can see just how close we are to the return of our Lord; that is to say, if you're looking for His return. As we have discussed earlier, Jesus pointed to past events to show where we are in our time frame. Such as the days of Noah and Lot, referring to how things were then and how they are now. It's with patterns of behavior that police are able to profile a person. Patterns are used in one form or another in every type of business known. Many businesses look at the spending patterns of the society to project what they will manufacture.

Our weather is forecasted by weather patterns. I am sure if some lady is reading this, she is probably thinking about a dress pattern. The list of patterns used in our daily life would probably fill a few pages.

The word *pattern* is used fourteen times in my Bible. All but two times it is used in describing the temple of God. The house of the Lord in Israel where the priest would approach the Holy of Holies. The pattern of the temple was laid out to be built in an exact way, as well as all the furnishings. In the fourteen times the word pattern is found, eleven times it is in the Old Testament, and three times in the New Testament. The first time we find the word pattern in the New Testament is in the Epistle of 1 Timimothy 1:16, where Paul mentions that He obtained mercy that in him, Jesus Christ might show a long suffering for a pattern to them who hereafter believe on Jesus for eternal life.

The word pattern is also found in the New Testament books of Titus and Hebrews. In Hebrews 8:5, it is talking about the pattern of the Old Testament temple and bringing it eventually into the new temple, which is you, as discussed in chapter 5 of this book. The plural use of *pattern* is found in Hebrews 9:23, tying up the use of the word *pattern* and telling us that we are that temple, covered by the blood of Jesus.

This pattern brings it all together, from the beginning to the end. We learn most everything through patterns. The last time any form of the word pattern is found, is in Hebrews 9:23. Why I find that interesting is that it ties all the previous uses of the word *pattern* together, as saying that we are that temple. This completes the temple. It brings the beginning and the ending together.

The reason I am writing about this, is to show you the importance of patterns. The other reason is to introduce you to the next chapter. I have found what I deemed to be an exciting chapter that is laid out in the history of the United States presidents. I see what I believe to be a definite pattern laid out that I believe you may also clearly see. I found through my study, that prior to my discovery there existed another study on a presidential pattern.

The pattern that was found had to do with a curse placed on our presidents by an Indian chief. In the next chapter I will also show you this curse by the Indian chief. I did find it to be of interest, but Proverbs 26:2, the Word of God, I think trumps a curse. It reads, *"The curse causeless shall not come."* Galatians 3:13 says, *"Christ has redeemed us from the curse of the law, being made a curse for us: for it is written, Cursed is every one that hangeth on a tree."*

In this chapter, we find that Jesus shows us a pattern in Luke 17:28,30, *"Likewise also as it was in the days of Lot. Even thus shall it be in the day when the Son of Man is revealed."* For more details read Genesis 19:5, *"And they called unto Lot and saith unto him. Where are the men, which came into thee this night? Bring them out unto us that we may know* [meaning sexually] *them."*

In late 2015, the Supreme Court overruled our Supreme God and allowed gay marriage. The Scriptures address this topic several times and call it an abomination in the sight of God.

In Leviticus 18:22, *"Thou shall not lie with mankind as with womankind: it is an abomination."*

Romans 1:27, *"And likewise the men, leaving the natural use of women, burned in their lust one toward another, men with men working that which is unseeingly and receiving in themselves the recompense of their error which was met."*

1 Corinthians 6:9, *"Know ye not that the unrighteous shall not inherit the Kingdom of God. Be not deceived neither formation nor violators, nor adulterers, nor effeminate, or abusers of themselves with mankind shall inherit the Kingdom God."*

Through what I have shown you here, I hope you see the importance of patterns in the Scriptures. We can possibly see what lays ahead by looking at patterns. Jesus told us to watch for things by showing us patterns of things that happened in the past will be repeated in the time he is to return. These things are found in the Gospels of Matthew, chapters 24 and 25, Mark, chapter 13 and Luke, chapters 17 and 21.

Isaiah 46:9–10 says, "Remember the former things of old: for I am God, and there is none else; I am God, and there is none like me. Declaring the end from the beginning, and from ancient times the things that are not yet done, saying, my counsel shall stand, and I will do all my pleasure."

Ecclesiastes 1:9 . . . "The thing that has been, is that which shall be; and that which is done, is that which shall be done."

Ecclesiastes 7:27 . . . "Behold, this have I found, saith the preacher, counting one by one, to find out the account."

CHAPTER NINE

POSSIBLE END-TIME-PRESIDENTIAL PATTERN

Isaiah 46:10, *"Remember the former things of old: for I am God, and there is none else; I am God, and there is none like me, Declaring the end from the beginning and from ancient times the things that are not yet done."*

Looking at the above verses, I believe there is unique pattern that shows us that our United States presidents have reached their end. And so it will be with our United States. They will no longer be if this pattern remains intact. Let's take a brief look at the last eight presidents and compare them to the first eight presidents and see if you can tell just what I'm talking about. I will be excluding President Obama, as he is currently holding this office. Like the above Bible verses and many other verses seem to indicate that we have signs that tell us Jesus is coming soon, (Times Up!)

The First Eighth US Presidents
George Washington
John Adams
Thomas Jefferson
James Madison
James Monroe
John Quincy Adams
Andrew Jackson
Martin Van Buren

The Last Eighth US Presidents
Lyndon B. Johnson
Richard M. Nixon
Gerald Ford
James Carter
Ronald Reagan
George H. W. Bush
William J. Clinton
George W. Bush

What is unique about the pattern of listed presidents is that they all completed their term in office before one died while holding this office. So here we have a list of eight consecutive living presidents who stepped down from their office. The eighth president, Martin Van Buren was the first president that was born in the United States. And if all current news is accurate about President Obama's birth certificate, that would mean that President George W Bush would be the last President born in the United States. From our first President, Washington, we never had a death to a sitting President until our ninth President, which was William H. Harrison. This brings us to the conclusion that as this date in the history of our US presidents, we have never had more than eight US Presidents that completed their term and stepped down from this office without a death to another president dying in between. I believe this shows a pattern of eight, as the number eight gives us the most US presidents that lived before a death came to that office and it just so happens that, that is the same number of presidents, as of this date that died in office.

Our current sitting President is the forty-fourth president. I find this interesting. Let me explain. We have covered earlier that the number 22 relates to prophecy. The number 22 x 2 = 44. President Obama is our forty-fourth president. From our first President to our forty-fourth there is 220 years of presidential history. That is the total number of years from President Washington to President Obama's election to office. The 220 years could be thought of as the number 22 if you discard the 0 behind the number 220. The reason I multiplied the number 22 with a 2 is that Scripture tells us we should have at least 2 witnesses for confirmation. I think that these numbers reveal something here. I am not saying that this is prophetic or prophecy, but I think this shows a pattern that seems to point to a period of time. Let's continue with the pattern of our presidents so I can show you what I am talking about. Going back from Washington to Van Buren, seen in the above list of the eight presidents, I would like to show what happens if we expand the list and we stretch it out and show a pattern of twelve presidents.

The ninth president from Washington was William H. Harrison, who died in office. After Harrison, we had two presidents serve and Taylor was our twelfth President. This sets a pattern. I will elaborate on this more, but at this time I would like to continue and show you still, another pattern. Our twelfth president, Taylor died in office. Taylor is a start to yet another pattern. After Taylor died in office, three presidents served and Lincoln died in office. After Lincoln, three presidents served and Garfield died in office. After Garfield, three presidents served and McKinley died in office in. After McKinley died, three presidents served and Harding died in office. That is five presidents who died, each separated by three presidents in between.

At first glance you may have missed this pattern, because President Cleveland, our twenty-second president, was also our twenty-fourth president; the only president to have served a split term. Another thing I find interesting is that President Cleveland, who was defeated Benjamin Harrison, the only grandson of a president to become president, also defeated Harrison to become the twenty-fourth president.

Before we continue, I would like to add that this has nothing to do with numerology. Take another look at Grover Cleveland, who was our twenty-second president after Washington and 22 presidents before our forty-fourth president, Barack Obama. As discussed, the number 22 is the number for revelation. Through the Bible we see that numbers seem to refer to a specific time or number or thought that contains a certain number of things. So continuing with this thought, I want to bring in a few more numbers that I think might show a pattern. Going back to the five presidents that died in office, each were separated by three living presidents.

This list contains four living presidents in between the five presidents that died while holding office. This brings us to the number four. Before I continue and show you more of these numbers involving the presidents, I would like to show you an example of what I discussed thus far with the importance of numbers and how they show us patterns in the Scriptures.

The number 5 is found many times in Scripture and numerically from patterns. Let's continue as I explain. The fifth chapter of Genesis shows us the generations from Adam to Noah. The fifth time Noah's name is mentioned it says Noah found grace. Another example is the five stones David used to defeat Goliath, or in Ephesians 4:11, *"And he gave some to apostles; and some prophets; and some evangelists; and some pastors_and teachers."* This is known in many churches as the fivefold ministry. The number 3 gives us the Godhead, as *"these three are one,"* Found in 1 John 5:7–8. There are many more times we are shown this pattern of three. Jesus rose from the grave on the 3rd day. The word numbers are only found 3 times in the Bible. The number 4 could point to the four Gospels or we can look at who our warfare is against, found in Eph. 6 where it mentions that are fight is against, *"Principalities, against Powers, against the rulers of the darkness of this world, against Spiritual Wickedness in high places."* The reason for the side track with the numbers and what they could possibly stand for is twofold, as it was with numbers such as counting things that I found this pattern. Second, I will be using these numbers to show yet, another pattern.

At this time, I would like you to see a pattern of twelve presidents and show just how similar they are when you compare the first twelve with the last twelve. I will start by making   a roll with the first president, George W. Bush, and continue down the row to the twelfth president. Opposite the first twelve presidents is a row of the last twelve presidents, with the last president stepping down from the office and going backward to the twelfth president. President Obama is not shown on the list as he still holds this office. I hope you can see just much these two rows compare when you look at them side by side. Also consider this verse from the Bible. Eccl. 1:9, *"The thing that hath been, it is that which shall be; and that which is done is that which shall be done."*

First 12 Presidents going backward		Last 12 Presidents going forward
George Washington		George W. Bush
John Adams		William Clinton
Thomas Jefferson		George H.W. Bush
James Madison		Ronald Reagan
James Monroe		Jimmy Carter
John Q. Adams		Gerald Ford
Andrew Jackson		Richard M. Nixon
Martin Van Buren		Lyndon B. Johnson
William H. Harrison	(died in office)	John F. Kennedy
John Tyler		Dwight D. Eisenhower
James K Polk		Harry S Truman
Zachary Taylor	(died on office)	Franklin D. Roosevelt

Looking at two lists above, you can see that both the first and the last presidents shared the same first name. Both Washington and Bush belonged to secret societies. Washington was initiated into the Freemasons and was a master mason and Bush was a member of the Skull and Bones. Each took a secret oath to belong to these societies. Going back to the two rows above I would like you to notice that each row has a father and son who held the office has president. You can also find that the same holds true if you narrow the list to eight presidents.

At this time, I would like for you to turn back to the list of the eight presidents and notice the sixth president is the son of a president, and in the second row the sixth president is the father of a president. I find this interesting insofar as the first row, or the beginning, is the son and the second row, the ending, is the father. Beginning with the young and ending with the old. I also found it interesting that both shared the same first names as their fathers. Not that it's uncommon to share your father's name, but both had other children with different names, but it was the ones who had the same name who shared the office. The list of the twelve presidents, I believe shows us a pattern of twelve, thus giving us another pattern of numbers to look at. As you can see, both the ninth and twelfth president died in office.

President Franklin Roosevelt was the only president to have held the office for twelve years. Recalling the sequence of the five presidents who died in office, each separated by three living presidents. Those three living presidents counted together total twelve. In our history, we have had exactly twelve presidents who served two complete terms and we had twelve presidents who served one complete term. Altogether, we note just how many times the number twelve pops up this way. Counting them out, first would be the twelve in the two rows above. I count this as two. The third twelve would be those twelve presidents found in between those five presidents that died. The fourth would be the three full terms that FDR served, twelve. The fifth would be the twelve presidents who served one complete term. The sixth would be the totaling 12 presidents who served two complete terms. If you remember, six is the number of man. The Bible reveals that the number twelve represents the government. For example, there are twelve tribes and there are the twelve apostles. Today we have mans' government, which in the very near future will be replaced by Gods' government. This is when Jesus rules and reigns on Earth for one thousand years.

Just where does our current president fit in? How does he fit in, if at all, to what the above patterns are showing us, *"The thing that hath been, is that which shall be."* The answer is, he doesn't fit any of the patterns. I will show you from the patterns above. First, there were only eight presidents who stepped down from office before a death came to a serving president. Second, eight presidents died while holding office; four were assassinated and four died of natural causes. We had twelve presidents who served one complete term and we had twelve presidents who served two complete terms. At this time President Obama is our ninth living President holding office, so what do I think is a likely scenario for our President? If he steps down from office, he will break the pattern of the twelve. If he dies in office, he will break the pattern of eight who died and he would also break the pattern of the eight living presidents.

What I think could happen, certainly the time is very likely, our president could declare martial law and remain in office. With various training exercises going on around our country with helicopters flying over cities and ground troops moving through the streets could be preparations for just such an event. We also have more police SWAT teams wearing military camouflage. Just how well is the camouflage working in our city streets? I mean it doesn't make them blend in with buildings. I don't think it is working. I believe the idea behind it is to make our military blend in with our police so we won't be so alarmed when we see them in our city streets.

Also, I would like to point out that our police now have military vehicles which were issued by our government. What's with that? You don't think that they just wanted us to get used to seeing them on our streets, do you? Another way our president could stay in office isn't any less terrifying. We could become the "North American Union." This would bring our current way of doing things into a whole new light. For instance, we would no longer have a president but a prime minister or king or whatever kind of title you hang on the ruler.

You might say, what is a North American Union? Back in 2005 our then-president, Bush, pushed for this. This is when Canada, Mexico, and our United States all become one country. NAFTA is the structure or start of just such a union. The North American Free Trade Act is a super highway between our three countries promoting free trade. This promoted the structure for the North American Union and our new government. Our country is not the same. 9/11 changed our country, and it continues to change day by day. If we look back in history to learn what will happen in the future, looking at Germany a man named Hitler was elected who was very charismatic who over time became a dictator, could this be a possibility here? After all, do I need to be concerned that this could happen here, in our country? Do I need to be concerned that my government is watching me? Do we have cameras almost everywhere watching people? Are our communications networks being listened to? Can we expect privacy on our home computers; are they being monitored? I know that God is watching and listening to me, but I am beginning to think that our government is trying to play God, and this has me very concerned. Our God said to pray for those who rule over us. I do pray for our leadership. This was once, at one time the greatest nation upon the face of the earth. I think our government is leading us purposely into a financial collapse, a one-world currency, a global government, a "New World Order."

There is yet another pattern with our presidents that I was not made aware of until well after I found the one I just shared with you. This pattern was brought about by our ninth president, William H Harrison. I will share with you of what I found about the curse from Wikipedia. The name of the curse is Curse of Tippecanoe, also known as **Tecumseh's Curse**, the **Presidential Curse**, **Zero Year Curse**, the **20-Year Curse,** or the **20-Year Presidential Jinx**. The curse, widely noted in a *Ripley's Believe It or Not* book published in 1931, began with the death of William Henry Harrison, who died in 1841 after being elected in 1840. For the next 120 years, presidents elected in years ending in zero (occurring every 20 years) ultimately died while serving in office, from Harrison to John F. Kennedy (elected 1960 died 1963).

The name "Curse of Tippecanoe" derives from the 1811 battle. As governor of the Indiana Territory, William Harrison used questionable tactics in the negotiation of the 1809 Treaty of Fort McHenry with Native Americans, in which they ceded large tracts of land to the US government. The treaty further angered the Shawnee leader, Tecumseh, and brought government soldiers and Native Americans to the brink of war in a period known as Tecumseh's War. Tecumseh and his brother organized a group of tribes designed to resist the westward expansion of the United States.

In 1811, Tecumseh's forces, led by his brother, attacked Harrison's army in the Battle of Tippecanoe, earning Harrison fame and the nickname, "Old Tippecanoe." Harrison strengthened his fame even more by defeating the British at the Battle of Thames during the War of 1812. In the account of the aftermath of the battle, Tecumseh's brother, Tenskwatawa, known as The Prophet supposedly set a curse against Harrison and future White House occupants who become President during years with the same end number as Harrison. This is the basis the curse legend. My take on this, is that Jesus took all curses to the cross and nailed them there. Proverbs 26:2b, ***"so the curse causeless shall not come."***

Returning to the pattern that I found and another that has the same idea of history repeating itself was discussed shortly after the assassination of President Kennedy. I did find this pattern interesting, as it shows the similarities of the first president assassinated and the last one to be assassinated. This shows to me a beginning and an ending. That is the same thing I have shown with the pattern I presented. President Kennedy was the last president that died in office and he was the last president who was assassinated. There were quite a few similarities shared with these two presidents, including their vice presidents.

After looking at the similarities, I found that not all of the listed similarities could be proved. I will list a couple that I found to be true and as far as I'm concerned showed a definite pattern. Lincoln was elected to Congress in 1846.

Kennedy was elected to Congress in 1946. Lincoln was elected President in 1860. Kennedy was elected President in 1960. Lincoln's vice president was Johnson and Kennedys' vice president was Johnson. Both vice presidents were born one hundred years apart. Andrew Johnson was born in 1808 and Lyndon Johnson was born in 1908. There was one other president who had a vice president named Johnson, and that was Martin Van Buren, our first president born in the United States. As stated earlier, there were other similarities that seem too trivial to mention, and there were some that were either untrue or could not be confirmed.

In todays' society we, as a people do not appreciate all that we have. Even if you are rubbing two nickels together you have it so much better than millions, or perhaps with our population, billions have it. Today we all seem to want our government to give us money for doing nothing to earn it. I remember when President Kennedy said at his inaugural speech, "Ask not what your country can do for you; ask what you can do for your country." That really impressed me as a young man. I thought to myself right at that moment, *when he runs for a second term, I'm going to vote for him*. Today everyone is asking their government to do for them, instead of asking what they can do for their country. The pride of providing for our families. Instead, we wait for our government to provide for us. We have been blessed with this great country, which I believe was supernaturally given to us by God, that we could do His will.

Today we seem to have turned a blind eye to God, as so many ungodly things are happening around us. We have had so many of God's warnings in our very face, yet we seem to be blind. I think decay has crept into our country. The people of this once-great nation don't want God's hand upon it. In fear that we might offend someone, God is not welcomed in schools, so He has been replaced by shootings. God is not welcomed in our workplace, so we have shootings there as well. Now God is not welcomed in our government, and what do we end up with? 9/11. I think it is because God is not welcomed in our country. Wake up, America! What if this pattern of presidents holds true and we have reached an end? Just something to consider.

I believe the first thing that our founding fathers who came here on the *Mayflower* did was drop to their knees on the shores of this land and thank God. If our current police state was around, then they would have been arrested for public worship. Going back to the pilgrims, I think you can see that it was the hand of God sustained them. Half of the pilgrims died through the first winter.

An unverified tale says that Squanto, an American Indian who a short time before had been taken by Englishmen to England, possibly for slave trading, was instead taught English, converted to Christ and brought back to America. The spring of the following year, he found the pilgrims. He taught them to fish, hunt, and plant and harvest corn. That fall they celebrated their first Thanksgiving. 2 Chronicles 7:14, ***"If my people, who are called by my name, shall humble themselves, and pray, and seek my face, and turn from their wicked ways, then will I hear from heaven, and will forgive their sins, and will heal their land."***

I would like to share one more thought with you. God chose Israel, this tiny little nation, this people. Through history, as we look at Israel, we know that other gods crept in and the people divided. This is when they no longer served the one true living God. Because of this, not only did the people become divided, but the land was divided as well. Because of this, nation and people split; therefore, they had a king over Israel and a king ruling over Judah. This all came about as the people left God. Israel has always been set apart for us to watch. If we watch the history of Israel and watch our Scriptures, we can see what will happen. We can look at the patterns and what the people and government did and see the outcome of their actions.

We have this same thing happening in our country today. We as a people no longer worship our living God. We're split, and I think we're losing our land. The Scriptures say in Isaiah 5:20, *"Woe unto them that call them that call evil good, and good evil; who put darkness for light, and light for darkness; who put bitter for sweet, and sweet for bitter!"* By the way, Israel had altogether forty-four kings, though some say 43. Either way, our current president is the 44th president but actually he could also be called the 43rd, as Cleveland, who had a split term, was counted twice. Today, we have unwanted babies being aborted, torn apart from their mothers' womb. At one time we called that an immoral act; it is now called right. Today wrong is right and right is wrong. God has given us many warnings. Let's take heed.

Matthew 5:9 . . . "Blessed are the peacemakers: for they shall be called the children of God."

CHAPTER 10

POLICE OFFICERS ACCORDING TO SCRIPTURES

As His children, He has provided guidance for the officer in the streets. If we look in the New Testament, we can see the Roman soldier, as he acted as the police officer in that day. The first soldier (the police officer) mentioned in the New Testament is mentioned in the book of Matthew 8:9, (This is speaking of a shift commander or sergeant, someone with rank who is talking to Jesus.) *"For I am a man under authority, having soldiers under me: and I say to this, Go, and he goeth; and to another, Come and he cometh; and to this servant Do this, and he doeth it."*

This first mention of this police officer was marveled at by Jesus as a man of great faith. This officer took Jesus at his word. He believed so much in him, that at his word, he said to Jesus, "You just say the word that my prayer is answered and I know it's a done deal." You may say that if Jesus was standing right before you, but I would say the same thing would apply by just reading His word. In the Gospel of John, in the first chapter, it says Jesus is the Word of God. Jesus said this to Thomas, in John 20:29, *"Thomas, because thou hast seen me, thou hast believed: Blessed are they that have not seen, and yet have believed."*

I recently came across a book that caught my eye with the title, *Cold–Case Christianity*. It was written by a homicide detective who worked cold cases. This detective was a known atheist who one day decided to read the Scriptures. Before I continue, note that I did not read his book. At this time, I have only glanced at the beginning and found it interesting. I do know he looked at the Bible like an investigative tool. He also looked at the people that Jesus communicated with and the many witnesses after He rose from the dead. He discovered that Jesus Christ was exactly who He was, God in the flesh. This book was authored by detective, J. Warner Wallace of the Torrance Police Department in Torrance California.

I became a Christian almost four years after I became a police officer. I worked for four different police departments over 35 years. I retired in 2011 and now serve as chaplain with three different police departments and one fire department. If you're a police officer don't get on me about being involved with a fire department; they are also a good bunch of people.

In my early years as a police officer, prior to my *born again* experience, I was king of the dirty jokes (at least I thought so). I would frequent the bar scene, wearing my T-shirt saying "Feel safe tonight, sleep with a cop." Today I would be ashamed to wear such a shirt. At that time of my life I was a good person who would have gone to heaven. At least that is what I thought. After all, I was a police officer who would arrest the bad. Though I didn't go to church, I knew

Jesus. At least I thought I did. I treated people well. Surely the scales were weighed in favor of my good works. I formed the idea that the good things that I did outweighed the bad. Never reading the Bible, I was totally ignorant of what God had to say. At that time, I never knew that no matter how good I was or thought I was, I could never be good enough or ever earn my way into heaven. I was doing like that Frank Sinatra song, doing it "my way." But the thing is, there is only one way to God. John 14:6, *"Jesus saith unto him, I am the way, the truth, and the life: no man cometh unto the Father, but by me."* He also said in John 3:3, *"Except a man being born again, he cannot see the kingdom of God."* I found out that God did care for me, and had I died, I would have ended in hell because I did not do what His Word said. God's Word is the law, and we have all said it at one time or another, ignorance to the law is no excuse.

For you officers working the streets, I would like to share a few verses I used while working the streets; one that a friend of mine uses to this day while he works the streets. At times he has to pull traffic on a Sunday. So many times he would come across a church member or clergy member who would throw their title at him and he had no quick response. I told him to remind that clergy of Romans (referring to the book of Romans) the 13th chapter tells you to obey the laws of the land. After he had said this to one particular clergy, the clergy hung his head and said, You're right, Officer," and more less thanked him for that reminder.

I know I had pretty much the same response when I was out there working the streets. I can't tell you how so many people thanked me personally for reminding them that God still cares. The phrase "Separation between church and state" wasn't meant to keep the church out of our government, but just the opposite. This was meant to keep our government out of the church. This is exactly what is happening today. The government has just about moved the church (Christian church) out of every building and public assembly hall today, but at the same time allows other religions into many more. You will be removed from a school if you bring a knife or a Jesus T-shirt into it.

The officer who used the Romans chapter of the Bible didn't say he was trying to convert anyone nor did he say the word *Bible*, which today seems to be another bad word. He simply said, "Romans 13 says, 'obey the laws of the land'." I don't think, at least as of this time, you can catch any flak for that. But then again, in this time that we're in, it seems things are worse than ever.

In todays' church, you can be in a lot of trouble if you preach certain things behind a pulpit, let alone say certain things on the street.

One thing to think about that was helpful to me is to remember that the person you are confronting isn't angry with you, the individual. This person is angry with the police office, the uniform that you're wearing, which represents authority. People are mostly proud and do not like being told what they can and cannot do, they don't like dealing with those who have authority over them. This is much like a child who has to deal with their parents. All through life you must deal with someone who has authority over you.

Going back to the 13th chapter of Romans, you will also learn that a police officer is actually a "minister" as described in the fourth verse of that chapter. This position that you have is ordained by God, and therefore comes a responsibly not just to the department you serve, but to   God.

In the New Testament book of Ephesians, we find in that the person who we are dealing with isn't really so much the problem. In the 6th chapter of that book, in verse 12, it tells us who we have to deal with. *"For we wrestle not against flesh and blood, but agains principalities, against powers, against the rulers of the darkness of this world, against spiritual wickedness in high places."*

In the 14th through the 17th verse of this chapter, it tells us how to equip ourselves with the "Armor of God." Verse 14, *"Stand therefore, having your loins girt about with truth, and having on the breastplate of righteousness;"*

Verse 15, *"And your feet shod with the preparation of the gospel of peace""*

Verse 16, *"Above all, taking the shield of faith, wherewith ye shall be able to quench all the fiery darts of the wicked."*

Verse 17, *"And take the helmet of salvation, and the sword of the Spirit, which is the word of God."*

As the apostle Paul looked at the Roman soldier, which was the police officer of that day, he made reference to his uniform with a spiritual application. Likewise, we can look at our uniforms today with the same application.

Let's convert the armor, looking at the picture below.

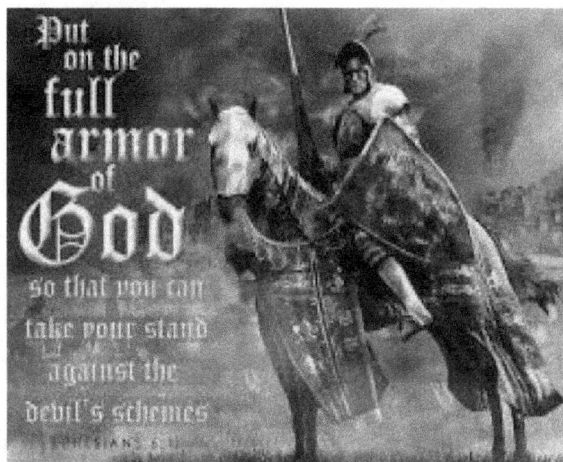

As we look above, around the soldier's midsection is a belt holding perhaps a sword and dagger. This is where Paul mentioned to have your loins girt about with truth. Today this would be your duty belt. The next item mentioned is the breastplate of righteousness. This can be compared to the badge of ones' authority. After this we find the feet shod with the preparation of the gospel, this would be your duty boots for foot protection.

After this is the shield of faith, quenching the fiery darts. This would describe your bulletproof vest. The next item is the helmet of salvation. This would be the hat which generally holds a badge, shield or the caption *POLICE* on it, or as pictured below a helmet with a department insignia on it. The last piece of armor mentioned is the Spirit which is the Word of God. The most deadly force for the police officer would be his handgun. This completes the officer's uniform, which symbolizes the Armor of God.

You will find that in the book of Psalms, chapter 91, to be an important one; one to be read often, especially before your tour of duty. This psalm is a psalm of protection. This chapter only has sixteen verses, but keep in mind it is Gods' Word; therefore, it has great power. This is a psalm of protection for both the fire fighters and the police. Read it often, memorize it, and keep it with you always. Like a familiar commercial says, "Don't leave home without it."

How many times do you go to a domestic and the first one who confronts you lets you know quite convincingly all that is wrong? Well, the Bible also addresses this as well. Prov. 18:17, *"He that is first in his own cause seemeth just; but his neighbor cometh and searcheth him."*

Another verse that I see to be important while dealing with the youth but also addresses the adults is found in Prov. 13:20, *"He that walketh with wise men shall be wise: but a companion of fools shall be destroyed.* "For this reason, I am careful for the company I keep to still apply to myself, who do I listen to or get advice from?

This next one I find important as we, as individuals, must remember, especially you officers in the streets today, as so many people and cameras are watching and/or recording your every move. This one you might think doesn't pack much punch, but believe me it works and has kept me out of trouble while I was still working the streets. Prov. 15:1, *"A soft answer turneth away wrath: but grievous words stir up anger.* "One thing you don't want to do is get into a shouting match, and you certainly do not want it to escalate into a brawl. I do know that at times it may seem that they can't hear you, you may raise your voice a bit but keep it as a "soft answer." After all, when you start yelling, not only do they become more angered, but it also generates anger in yourself. One other thing is working against you in all of this: it's the uniform, that symbol of authority that they already do not like, so you have that going against you to start with.

You will find that this book of Proverbs addresses much of how to handle yourselves on the street, after all Prov. 20:24 says, *"Man's goings are of the LORD; how can a man then understand his own way?"*

The book of Proverbs has thirty-one chapters in it. This gives you one chapter to read each day of the month. Put this on your things to do list. It's a wealth of information.

As with the direction of this book before we came to this chapter, it's what I believe the police officer is heading into and may not be aware of. I think that it may be quite possible that we are heading into not just a police state, but police country. It starts slow, like all transactions do. What I see happening according to Scripture is the police office to become more military-like. If that scenario doesn't happen, perhaps the National Guard will overrun everything. This is more or less what happened during Hitler's reign. The military was patrolling the streets while Hitler was the dictator running everything. Perhaps the police officer might be replaced by the military soldier.

More and more today we see our police officers being armed with military-type vehicles and the swat teams uniformed in military-type clothing. What's with that? Are we being conditioned for a possible takeover by our military to patrol our streets? I did see recently, on one of the news channels what looked like a paramilitary drill, with helicopters flying over a busy West Coast highway firing blanks in the nighttime hours. I must say, what's with this? It looked like one of those action movies. I also learned of a town actually made just for such drills with military soldiers on the ground performing military operations. Is this maybe a drill for a coming martial law?

We all watched with horror what happened at the Boston Marathon. What we were told was that a couple of jerks set off a bomb at the finishing line. I'm not sure if that's exactly how it went down, as I received this news from our government. I believe that today much of our news media is spoon-fed to us via the government. That is only a thought of mine, so please don't let it govern your affairs.

This is where we are today. So many crazy things happening, and we receive so many lies from the mouths of our government spokespeople. No wonder I think the way I do. Getting back to this incident in Boston, we came under martial law here in the good old USA. Who would have expected to see that? Not only did it happen, but just realize this: nothing much was said about it. Homeowners were removed from their homes as police officers were directed to make unwarranted searches through each home. Is this something that will happen again, maybe soon? We just touched on that possibility in the last chapter.

Speaking of this incident that occurred in Boston, I sometimes wonder just how much of this is how it happened or was this just something that was generated to make us feel okay with martial law. After what happened in Benghazi, I see what could be possibly cover-ups of many of todays' happenings. It's something like a Mel Gibson move I saw named *Conspiracy Theory*. I sometimes think I am overreacting to so much, and yet I still wonder, because there is just so much happening. I really don't recognize this country as the country I grew up in. Please pray for our country and our leaders. And mostly don't forget to put on the "Armor of God."

NOTES

All Scripture listed and referenced throughout this book are from the King James Bible.

CHAPTER 1

Wikipedia, History of Magic Squares. "The GREAT SEAL OF THE UNITED STATES, Its History, Symbolism and message for the New Age by Paul Foster Case, Copyright, 1935 Pastor Michael Hoggard, teaching on the number 13. The number 13 on the dollar found in "The Great Seal of the United States, by Paul Foster Case.

> Bohemian Grove, Explaining The Giant Owl, Wikipedia Phoenix Mythology. Explaining the Egypt Mystical Bird Jewish Mysticism, The Kabbalah, leading to the number 72.

CHAPTER 2

> Pastor Michael Hoggard, teaching on Bible Numerology, numbers relating to scriptures
> *The Divine Code, From One to 2020: Numbers, Their Meanings and Patterns* by Steve Cioccolanti (Creation House).
> Operation Paperclip. Although there are numerous books on this topic, I received my information from Wikipedia which is so readily available.

DARPA, information came from several sources such as Infowars, WND, and the Drudge Report to name a few.
CERN hadron collider, http://phys.org/news/2011-03-large-headron-collider-world-machine.html.

CHAPTER 3

Stanley R Mickelsen Safe Complex http://www.weather.com/news/stanley-r-mickelsen-safe-guard-complex-pyramid-build-middle-nowhere-20140420.

Adullam Films, *Riddles in Stone* documentary from http://www.adulmfilms.com.

Washingtonople, The Secret History of Americas Capital by Conrad Yates, http://www.bibliotecapleyades.net/esp_exopolitics_ZBhtm#menu.

Apollyon Rising 2012 by Thomas Horn (Defender , 2009)

Capital Secrets by Michael Hoggard.

CHAPTER 4

The Divine Code, From One to 2020: Numbers, Their Meanings and Patterns by Steve Cioccolanti (Creation House).

Petrus Romanus, The Final Pope Is Here by Tom Horn and Cris Putman (Defender, 2012)

Jesus Christ, DNA and the Holy Bible by Mike Hoggard.

Mcfadden-Bush interview, Bush, God the Bible and Universalism on YouTube.

Gibson Bush interview, Bush, God the Bible and Universalism on YouTube.

CHAPTER 5

Jesus Christ, DNA and the Holy Bible by Mike Hoggard.

CHAPTER 6

The Complete Book of Numerology by Joyce & Jack Keller (London: St. Martin's Griffin, 2012).

Little Giant Encyclopedia of Numerology by Daniel Heydon (Sterling, 2005).

Your Days Are Numbered by Florence Campbell (DeVorss & Company, 1983).

The Secret Science of Numerology by Shirley Lawrence (New Page Books, 2001).

The Numbers Book by Sepharial (London: W Foulsham & Co Ltd, 1957).

CHAPTER 7

Fukushima Daiichi nuclear disaster, Wikipedia, http//www.wikipedia.org/ 2011 Tohoku earthquake and tsunami, Wikipedia, http//www.wikipedia.org/

Historical Events for Year ####, Historyorb.com Attack on Pearl Harbor, Wikipedia, http//Wikipedia.org/

CHAPTER 8

The Authorized King James Bible

CHAPTER 9

Teachings from Pastor Michael Hoggard

Curse of Tippercanoe-http//www.wikipedia.org/ Lincoln-Kennedy coincidences urban legend from Wikipedia, http//www.wikipedia.org/

CHAPTER 10

The Authorized King James Bible

As chaplain of three police departments and a fire department, I found what I thought to be a unique way to communicate with them. This book is a byproduct of that way. I also believe it to be a way to reach a person like you, the average person who sees all the unusual things that are occurring in this world today, and wonder where it will all end. This book is about such things. In this book will look learn from the following chapters,

ITS TIME, OUR DAYS ARE NUMBERED
SIGNS
HIDDEN NUMBERS IN STRUCTURES
NUMBERS IN THE BIBLE
MAN, THE TEMPLE OF GOD
NUMEROLOGY
EVENTS AND DATES POSSIBLY REVEALING
END TIMES PATTERNS
POSSIBLE END-TIME PRESIDENTAL PATTERN
POLICE OFFICERS ACCORDING TO
SCRIPTURES

In these thought-provoking chapters I think you will see just how short time is. I also think you will have a new respect for your KJV Bible.